JU

Martial R
POS **Tel: 019** HAVIOUR MANAGEMENT

28

14 | 1

21 - 1

22 F

04

Wessex Educational
Resource Centre
King Alfred's College,
Winchester SO22 4NR
Telephone: (0962) 62281

19

0 7

To be r

2006

Positive Behaviour Management

A Manual for Teachers

P.L. Cheesman and P.E. Watts

CROOM HELM
London & Sydney

NICHOLS PUBLISHING COMPANY
New York

© 1985 P.L. Cheesman and P.E. Watts

Croom Helm Ltd, Provident House, Burrell Row,
Beckenham, Kent BR3 1AT

Croom Helm Australia Pty Ltd, First Floor,
139 King Street, Sydney, NSW 2001, Australia

British Library Cataloguing in Publication Data

Cheesman, P.L.
    Positive behaviour management: a manual for
    teachers.
    1. Problem children—Education. 2. Behaviour
    modification
    I. Title II. Watts, P.E.
    371.93   LC4801

    ISBN 0-7099-3451-3
    ISBN 0-7099-3464-5 Pbk

First published in the United States of America 1986 by
Nichols Publishing Company, Post Office Box 96, New York, NY 10024

Library of Congress Cataloging in Publication Data

Cheesman, P.L.
    Positive behavior management.
    Bibliography: p.
    Includes index.
    1. Classroom management. 2. Behavior modification.
I. Watts, P.E. II. Title.
LB3013.C469   1985   371.1'024   85-8850
ISBN 0-89397-227-4
ISBN 0-89397-228-2 (pbk.)

Filmset by Mayhew Typesetting, Bristol, England
Printed and bound in Great Britain
by Billing & Sons Limited, Worcester.

CONTENTS

ACKNOWLEDGEMENTS

We gratefully acknowledge the help received from the following people for their valuable contributions to this book: Frances Croome for her accurate typing and unfailing patience; Brigid Foster-Watts for the ideas and artwork for the self-recording charts; Andy Ross for the cartoons in 'Ten Points to Remember'.

Peter Cheesman
Phil Watts

INTRODUCTION

This book is written with the aim of helping teachers to deal with those behaviour problems which are commonly encountered in the classroom and around the school. The term 'behaviour' is used in its widest sense and refers to any action carried out by a pupil. It could be concerned equally with unacceptable 'acting out' behaviour by an adolescent, or failure of a junior-aged child to work consistently, or the reluctance of a nursery-aged child to speak to adults. The techniques which are set out in the following chapters have been applied successfully to a vast range of different problems occurring in all types of school from nurseries to secondary schools, and in various forms of provision for pupils with special educational needs.

Many teachers think that it can be difficult to change children's behaviour. Sometimes it is! However, there are ways which can make it a much simpler and more enjoyable process for both teacher and pupil. This book offers a practical and easy-to-follow system that can be applied to almost any problem behaviour.

We have between us many years' experience in different types of school, both as teachers (one of us as a headteacher) and in our present work as educational psychologists. As psychologists we are in daily contact with teachers who have children with behaviour difficulties in their classes. The methods presented in this book have evolved from the application of theoretical psychological concepts to the problem behaviours of the children referred to us. One important objective for us is to provide practical advice and guidance to teachers.

The teacher, or in some cases the team of teachers, has always been the crucial agent of intervention, with the psychologist acting in an advisory capacity. A disadvantage of this way of working arises from the need to explain the relatively complex theoretical underpinning of the method every time a teacher is first introduced to it. Mounting in-service courses does, to some extent, deal with this problem. However, even this still leaves teachers without ready access to reference material that would reinforce their own learning and help them to deal quickly with difficulties.

This book has been written with the intention of filling this gap. The systematic, step-by-step approach adopted should provide teachers with a text from which to learn the basic concepts associated with the method, and one that will, at the same time, act as a working manual to refer to as a particular programme proceeds.

We have been at pains to ensure that the practice recommended is supported by the appropriate theory. However, at the same time, we have endeavoured to limit the theoretical material in order to prevent the practical concepts from becoming obscured.

The type of approach adopted in this book is not new, but unlike many of the presentations of behaviour modification we have sought to place our greatest emphasis upon the positive nature of the method. We firmly believe that children, like adults, respond much more effectively, readily and happily to an ethos which is positive and rewarding than they do to one which is punitive or authoritarian. We also firmly believe that fewer problems are generated in schools where the approach is firm and consistent but relaxed and positive. There is also a growing body of evidence to support this belief.

The book is divided into three main parts. The first discusses the main approaches which have been adopted over time to children's behaviour problems. The second part deals with assessment of behaviour. The third part discusses intervention strategies. The chapters that comprise Parts 2 and 3 each deal with just one aspect of the procedure under discussion. A step-by-step guide is provided in the form of an assessment chart or intervention chart to enable a teacher to design a behaviour management programme. Each chapter contains all the practical information necessary for the completion of a cell in either the assessment chart or the intervention chart. The appropriate chart is given at the beginning of each chapter and the cell with which it is concerned is clearly indicated. For further clarification of the technique a cumulative worked example is included with the charts, which illustrates the step-by-step approach that we have adopted.

Objectives of this Book

The objectives given below can be achieved by careful reading of this book. The reader should then be able to:

(1) define behaviour objectively;
(2) select the appropriate method of measuring the behaviour and implement this;
(3) identify the controlling factors of behaviour;
(4) select an appropriate target for change;
(5) select an appropriate means for intervention;

(6) monitor the progress of the intervention;
(7) decide if any changes are required in the intervention and implement these.

PART 1:

BACKGROUND TO BEHAVIOUR PROBLEMS

1 PSYCHOLOGICAL APPROACHES TO PROBLEM BEHAVIOUR

The writings of early psychologists such as Freud, Jung and others have had a tremendous influence upon the explanations put forward to account for human behaviour. It is not intended here to attempt to summarise the enormous body of theory that has been developed by these psychologists, but there are two generalisations that arise from the theories which should be discussed at this stage.

First, they proposed that the basic personality traits, individual drives and motivations are laid down during childhood as a consequence of the child-rearing practices adopted and the child's early experience. Secondly, the behaviours that are produced by an individual merely represent symptoms or subconscious mechanisms of which there is little or no awareness.

It can readily be seen from the above that in order to bring about changes in behaviour, the teacher would be faced with dealing with variables over which neither he nor the child can exercise control. This, not surprisingly, has often led to the view that many problems require the application of expertise and knowledge which it would be unreasonable to expect the ordinary teacher to possess, e.g. psychotherapy or play therapy.

Thus, traditional 'internal' causation approaches frequently explain behaviour in terms of personality factors. A child may be cheeky to his teacher and may hit other children because he has a hostile, aggressive personality. Alternatively, he may be perceived as disobedient because he cannot retain instructions due to poor intellectual ability. As this 'depth' psychology approach places its emphasis mainly on the environment of the past, it implies that there is little that can be done to change the child's current behaviour. For example:

'Susan won't do anything for herself.'

'Well, what do you expect? She is an only child and has been spoilt for a long time.'

This is an explanation of why Susan behaves in a certain way but gives no indication of what to do about it.

The approach with which we shall concern ourselves in this book looks at factors 'outside' the child: his present social environment, his home, his situation in school, and the relationship between the child and his peers and between the child and his teachers, the emphasis being firmly on the present environment. The crucial difference between the two approaches is immediately apparent. There is relatively little that can be done in any direct manner about the 'within' factors but at least some of the 'outside' factors are amenable to change.

In adopting our chosen approach and rejecting the traditional, we are not seeking to deny that past events do play a part in determining some aspects of current behaviour but rather we are questioning how useful these ideas are when faced with situations where practical and constructive actions are needed.

The alternative to the 'internal causation model' is based on learning theory, and approaches behaviour problems in a rather different way. It assumes that the 'causes' of any type of behaviour problem may lie in either the past or present environment of the child but that it is the *present environment* of the child that *maintains* these behaviours. It is central to our positive behaviour management approach that the opposite side of the same coin applies; namely, that if the present environment ceased to maintain the behaviours, they would disappear, or at least be reduced.

It assumes that the word 'problem' is just a social label attached to the behaviour and that the child *learns* his problem behaviour in just the same way that he learns every other behaviour. The same laws of learning apply to any behaviour — problem or otherwise — as they do to the learning of skills and information. Therefore, a child behaves in a certain way because he has learned, or been taught to behave in that way or because he has not been taught to behave differently. In short, almost all behaviour is learned. Hence behaviour, appropriate or inappropriate, can be taught, and, in the school situation, can be in the control of the teacher.

A child learns that if he completes his work his teacher is pleased. A child also learns that if he doesn't, the teacher may be cross. One behaviour he will repeat often and the other seldom, if at all. It is the behaviour of his teacher that has taught him. At least, that is the plan!

Positive Behaviour Management

One of the least satisfactory features of a great deal of educational innovation is the paucity of evaluative studies of the effects of new techniques and approaches. It is also true that few of the methods adopted to bring about behavioural change have been an integral part of any approach. Of those that have been set up with a clear intention to carry out evaluation as part of the process, the vast majority are within the field of behaviour modification. There are, in addition to these, a number of research studies which have evaluated existing procedures on criteria which the researchers themselves have set up. Topping (1983) has carried out a comprehensive review of dozens of such studies, and his general conclusion, based on the findings of these, is that the only consistently successful interventions are those that rely on some variety of behaviour modification.

Although the concern of this book is with children in the ordinary classroom, it is interesting to note that in the field of psychotherapy similar conclusions to those of Topping are drawn by Rachman (1971) in his review of the effectiveness of psychotherapy. The most telling point he makes is that two-thirds of patients who are referred for some form of disturbed behaviour cease to demonstrate their symptoms after a relatively short time even if nothing is done for them at all! In other words there is a 'spontaneous remission' rate of about 60 per cent. For any treatment to achieve a satisfactory level of effectiveness it must, clearly, have a success rate higher than this. As was the case in those studies carried out in education, the only treatments that did better than the spontaneous remission rate were those based on behaviour modification principles.

Many readers of this book will have come across the term 'behaviour modification' and it is possible that some will have already concluded that our term 'positive behaviour management' is merely a euphemism for this. Certainly, behaviour modification and positive behaviour management share the same underlying theoretical concepts, but we would argue that our approach represents the development of a much less mechanistic and more positive strategy towards behaviour change than has frequently been the case in the application of behaviour modification.

Criticism has been levelled at the methods of behaviour modification, focusing on the alleged failure of the approach to take account of individual differences and its mechanistic application. Perhaps this criticism has at times been justified, but to a considerable extent it may be a reflection of some of its practitioners rather than the practice itself. Paradoxically, it is the success of behaviour modification as a therapy which has led to some of its more extreme distortions. Because it has been so unusually effective in some hitherto intractable fields, e.g. the education of severely mentally handicapped children, it has been fastened upon by a range of workers in 'caring professions' who have applied the method enthusiastically and, at times, indiscriminately. Positive behaviour management is designed to overcome the objections of mechanistic approaches. It is a system that teachers can easily assimilate and use in their daily teaching.

To return to the reason why we have coined the term 'positive behaviour management', perhaps this is best explained by some examination of the use of the terms 'positive' and 'management'.

It is very often the case that when a child produces some form of unacceptable behaviour the focus of the action taken to change it, by teachers or by parents, is on the behaviour itself. Frequently, this takes the form of telling the child to stop producing the behaviour or of making threats regarding the consequences to the child if the behaviour is continued.

The 'positive' approach shares the same aim of attempting to bring about change in the unacceptable behaviour, but it differs from what is described above in that the focus is taken away from that behaviour and placed on a *different behaviour* where the endeavour is to bring about a greater occurrence in its frequency and/or duration.

The 'positive' approach is much more concerned with encouraging a child *to do* something rather than on instructing him to *stop doing* something.

Another aspect of the 'positive' approach is that the teacher or the parent is urged to be on the lookout for acceptable behaviour and to ensure that this does not pass unnoticed. The experience of most children is that it is possible to behave well, work consistently, do homework, help at home and do all the other things that adults seem to expect, without ever hearing a word of praise or positive encouragement for producing such behaviour. It is also their common experience that you only have to get out of line by an inch to become the focus of immediate attention! Our aim is to persuade our readers to reverse this situation.

So much for the term 'positive'. Our other chosen word 'management' we believe to have more positive connotations than the term 'modification'. The latter implies a passive subject who is having things done to him by others who know best. We use the term 'management' because in our view this implies at least an element of co-operation between the manager and those being managed. Workshops, offices, schools and homes where the 'managers' discuss the work being undertaken and consult with the 'workers' regarding decisions being taken invariably operate more efficiently and, at the same time, are the source of much greater satisfaction to all those involved in them than those where consultation is non-existent and decisions are made without reference to those who will be affected by them. In our approach the term 'management' implies the active involvement of the child in bringing about behaviour change, and regular consultation and discussion with him about the way things are going.

Positive behaviour management is about partnerships, the acquisition of independence and the development of self-monitored control.

It will very soon become apparent to those who read this book that to apply the principles of positive behaviour management successfully requires minute attention to detail, an awareness of all the factors leading up to and following upon behaviours and a degree of flexibility in dealing with different situations which we would argue is not commonly found in schools or any other institutions. It is this attention to detail wherein lies the success of this system. It is unfortunate that a cursory examination of the concepts can lead to the belief that it is nothing much more than the application of 'common sense', and it is, therefore, perfectly justifiable to apply the method without wasting too much time on study. A significant amount of the content of this book will, we hope, be recognised by teachers as 'common sense' but we hope also that it will be recognised that it is being applied in a very systematic manner. There is a need to study the method carefully, as interventions based on an incomplete understanding of the method will surely encounter difficulties. It is likely that the failure may then be attributed to the method rather than the user.

A more difficult matter to deal with is the philosophical one which questions the ethical justification of using a powerful system to change an individual's behaviour. This is worthy of serious discussion but this book is not the appropriate vehicle for entering into a philosophical debate. However, we would contend that all institutions engage in behaviour change, at times perhaps unknowingly. If this is the case, then it is surely better to be aware of what is being done, with specified targets stated, than to be engaged in what may be not much more than a random exercise. A key aspect of positive behaviour management is the participation of the pupil in the change process. This overcomes to a large extent the rightful criticism of 'doing things to children'. The pupil becomes a partner in the process, helping to decide on both the direction of change and the method used to bring it about. It is essential that behaviour change be seen as a partnership.

This book presents a consistent theoretical framework and method for implementation. It will be helpful for the reader if, at this stage, we summarise the underlying assumptions of our approach.

(a) Most childhood behaviour problems are simply excesses or deficits of behaviours that are common to all children. For example, most children lose their temper at one time or another. It may become a problem if it is happening every day. Similarly, all children, when very young, are not toilet trained. This is not a problem: it is part of natural child development. However, it might be regarded as a problem if the child was 12 years old. Behaviour should only be regarded as a problem if it is inappropriate for the child or not in his best interests having regard to his age, development, situation and others to whom he relates.

(b)   The term 'problem behaviour' is a social label. As suggested in (a), behaviour is regarded as a problem if it is not 'normal' for a child of that age and development in a particular situation. What is normal? To judge this, account must be taken of the norms and expectations of the child, his family, his friends, his class, school and wider society. The teacher should also take into account whether her own expectations and standards are colouring the expectations placed on the child.

(c)   All behaviour is learned. Behaviour that has not been learned can be taught. Behaviour that is happening to excess can be unlearned and more appropriate behaviour substituted.

(d)   Such learning must be within a social context. Problem behaviour cannot be changed in isolation from the situation where it is perceived as a problem. Learning is faster in a social environment because of the rewards, punishments and other models of appropriate behaviour that are available to the child.

(e)   Therefore, the teacher is the most appropriate change agent within schools. All teachers are informal changers of behaviour and indeed are doing so every day. They spend considerable amounts of time in direct contact with children. Teachers are in a much better position than visitors to schools such as psychologists, social workers, etc. They are in the position of giving praise and encouragement, giving or withholding attention, punishing, giving approval, etc.

(f)   Behaviour management techniques provide the teacher with an effective method of changing behaviour, incorporating many aspects of 'good teaching practice'.

(g)   Behaviour management is positively based. It assumes that change can occur and that it will be positive and an improvement for the child and those to whom he relates.

(h)   Behaviour management is about changing behaviour, not children. We are dealing with problem behaviour *not* problem children. They are only regarded as a problem because of the behaviour that they produce! This is a very important distinction.

(i)   Behaviour management is *not* doing things *to* children. It is

doing things *with* children, and their parents and any other significant people in the child's life. The child and others should be seen
as full and valued partners in the entire change process.

(j)   Prevention (or at least early intervention) is better than cure. At
first glance the procedures in this book may look lengthy and time
consuming. The first time it is tried, that may be the case. They
are meant to deal with difficult as well as straightforward problems. However, with practice, many of the methods can become
part of everyday teaching and can be applied to more minor problems, thus acting in a preventative manner.

We are now ready to proceed with exploring positive behaviour
management.

References

Rachman, S. (1971) *The Effects of Psychotherapy*, Pergamon, London
Topping, K.J. (1983) *Educational Systems for Disruptive Adolescents*, Croom Helm, London

2 FACTORS AFFECTING BEHAVIOUR

As we have already seen, there are a great many factors that can influence the behaviour of a child. In Chapter 1 it was suggested that a useful way of categorising these factors was to determine whether they were external to the child, i.e. aspects of the environment, or internal, i.e. aspects of the child's own physical and mental make-up. A further subdivision can also be made by considering the extent of the influence we are able to exert over these factors.

Clearly, there are some factors external to the child that teachers are able to change. Among these would be the curriculum, the classroom setting and the teacher's own approach to the child. Beyond the control of the teacher would be much of the home environment, although contact between school and home might have some effect here. The peer-group environment in some respects might also be largely beyond the control of the teacher, especially outside school hours.

The internal factors of temperament and personality may change to some extent in the long term but it would be very difficult confidently to ascribe such changes as being due to the effect of a school or a teacher. Similarly, physical factors would normally be admitted as being beyond the direct control of teachers.

In considering the brief summary of causation factors given above, it would seem that there are many more factors outside the control of the school than those which might respond to intervention. So many reasons are put forward by teachers and other professionals to explain problem behaviour, and because of the multiplicity of these 'causes' it is often so difficult to decide where to begin in order to bring about change that the whole endeavour is seen as hopeless. This may lend to the acceptance of difficult behaviour and, consequent upon this, confirmation in the mind of the pupil that such behaviour is permitted. Rather than accept this, we need to carry out a detailed analysis of the behaviour and the environment in which it occurs. As a first step it is important to focus our attention on those factors over which we can exert some influence.

All the following statements have been offered by teachers and other professionals as causes of problem behaviour in various pupils. It is instructive to rate each of these according to the extent of the influence the teacher or the school has over the cause of the problem behaviour. Note that in most cases the teacher may have some influence over the *effect* that each has, but concentration for this exercise should be focused on the cause.

Rate: 0 = no influence; 1 = some influence; 2 = much influence

Rating

(1)   Low intellectual ability.
(2)   Epileptic.
(3)   Ten children in family, father not working at present.
(4)   Aggressive, unsettled personality.
(5)   Only accepted by peers when 'acting the fool'.
(6)   Class sometimes unsupervised at the beginning of lessons.
(7)   Unsettled home background.
(8)   Difficulty with reading the texts used in class.
(9)   No interest in some subjects.
(10) Worksheets in some subjects too difficult.
(11) Inadequate attention span.
(12) Younger brother very successful in school.
(13) Lack of motivation.
(14) Parents do not care about John's situation in school.
(15) John's parents are divorced.
(16) Few achievements in school.
(17) Often seeks confrontation situations with teachers.
(18) Poor fine-motor skills.
(19) John was in the care of Social Services for three years.
(20) Forgets to bring equipment to lessons.

Implementing the Positive Behaviour Management Approach

Parts 2 and 3 of this book are designed to guide the reader through a detailed sequence of steps which should be followed when implementing positive behaviour management. These are now summarised. Included with each step is information regarding the location in the book of the chapters that are pertinent to it.

Step 1 (Chapters 3 and 4)

Decide exactly what is the problem in terms of:

(a)   the actual behaviour(s) — an accurate description;
(b)   its extent and seriousness;
(c)   a measurement of either its frequency or duration.

Step 2 (Chapter 5)

Decide on the priorities of the situation, i.e. what do you want to change?

Step 3 (Chapter 6)

Decide what are the environmental factors preceding and following the behaviour.

Step 4 (Chapter 7)

Decide what you want to happen instead.

Step 5 (Chapters 8 to 12)

Decide how to change the environment (pupil, work, teacher, class, etc.) in order to make the desirable behaviour(s) more likely to occur.

Step 6 (Chapter 13)

Monitor the progress of the intervention, making changes where necessary and then phasing them out.

PART 2:

ASSESSMENT OF BEHAVIOUR PROBLEMS

3 DESCRIBING BEHAVIOUR

Figure 3.1: Assessment Chart. Describing Behaviour

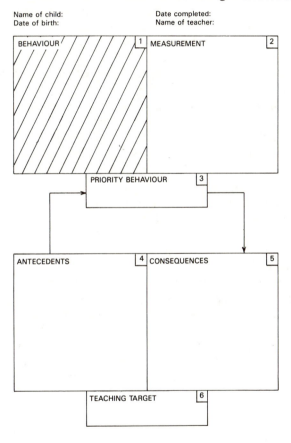

Aims

This chapter is concerned with looking at behaviour in such a way that its description is objective and not open to misinterpretation. This will allow the behaviour to be measured accurately. After reading this chapter you will be able to complete the 'behaviour' box (No. 1) of the assessment chart in Figure 3.1.

Describing Behaviour

The first stage in using a behaviour management approach is to describe behaviour in a clear, precise way. Once described it can then be observed and measured easily.

We often hear teachers and other professionals using neat but vague phrases to describe a child. For example, 'John is very disruptive, almost maladjusted', or 'Mary has a very poor self-image'. As statements these may (or may not) summarise what a worried teacher is feeling about a child but they do not help us to proceed in dealing with the behaviour, that is to say, promoting what is acceptable and reducing inappropriate behaviour.

The problem that arises from the use of such terms as 'maladjusted' or 'disruptive' is that these carry the implication that there is something wrong within the child which could be cured if only we could find the right treatment. This represents the medical model approach which serves only to divert attention away from those aspects of causation over which teachers may have some control. Using such terms may be a convenient shorthand but they do not advance our useful knowledge of the child in any way. This is well illustrated by the lack of agreement between the definitions that have been advanced for these categories. Put a group of teachers, psychologists, psychiatrists, social workers, etc., together and ask each of them to write a definition of a 'disruptive' child, and the likelihood is that as many different definitions would be produced as there were members in the group. To some the word could refer to a child producing behaviour as trivial as occasionally failing to raise his hand before answering a question, whereas to others it might typify a child who produces unprovoked and seemingly random physical attacks on his peers.

If we are to progress towards the kind of knowledge that will enable us to make decisions as to what can be done to alleviate the behaviours, then we must have *precise* descriptions of what it is the child actually does or does not do. The temptation to talk about behaviour in such obscure ways arises because often the child produces a series of behaviours which are then lumped together under one label. It is far more valuable to list each separate behaviour than to use one word which purports to cover all relevant behaviours. By so doing, the problem of these labels meaning different things to different people is avoided.

In adopting this approach we are able to start our analysis of the child's problem with a list of behaviours that need to be changed rather than some vague idea of changing the child. We start our intervention on the assumption that the acquisition of appropriate behaviours comes about through teaching and training in much the same way that other skills are taught. Consider the following more precise descriptions of the behaviour of children who have been labelled 'disruptive' and it will become immediately apparent that such descriptions could provide useful information to guide intervention.

'He's disruptive' may mean:

(a) When the class is quietly working he leaves his seat and walks around class.
(b) He goes to a group of children who are working and talks to them.
(c) He hits or prods other children and when they retaliate he calls out.
(d) He arrives late to lessons.
(e) He frequently taps his ruler on his desk, etc., etc.

Here are some further examples of what we might call vague or 'woolly' statements which have been redefined.

Vague statement	*Redefinition*
'He won't play nicely.'	If left unsupervised, takes toys from other children and refuses to share them.
'She is unable to concentrate.'	She works for no more than five minutes before leaving her seat and starting a conversation with another child.
'She is very shy.'	She talks to other children in the nursery but will not talk to any adults.

A good description of behaviour requires objectivity on the part of the observer and it takes practice to develop this skill. For the purposes of behaviour management, behaviour is: *what the child does that we can see*. It does not include any reference to motives or intentions for we cannot see them, i.e. 'Jason kicked Amanda', but *not* 'Jason kicked Amanda deliberately and maliciously.'

A good test of the objectivity of a description of behaviour would be the ability of two observers to make the same independent judgement that the behaviour had occurred.

Often in a vague description the adjectives used are open to many interpretations. A list of such words is given below and it would be wise to avoid the use of these when producing a description of behaviour which is to provide the foundation for objective measurement.

Avoid

Maladjusted Immature Disruptive Withdrawn Hyperactive
Acting out Noisy Lack of concentration Sulky Disrespect-
ful Attention seeking Unco-operative

In addition, the verb used is also often open to many interpretations. Here is a non-inclusive list of some verbs to be used and those to be avoided:

To be Used

Says Picks up Writes Takes apart Runs Shouts Cries Kicks
Hits Smiles Walks Copies Points to

To Avoid

Knows Understands Concentrates Learns Appreciates Infers
Recognises Resents Behaves

The crucial difference between these two sets of verbs is that the set that is recommended for use when describing behaviour refers to actions that may be observed. This is not the case with the other set. For example, it would be difficult to actually see a child 'inferring' and it would be even more difficult to obtain agreement between observers that it was taking place!

The redefinitions that you make will be different for different children and will refer *only to that child*. To redefine a vague statement we need to ask:

'What would I *see* happening when Fred is being [disruptive, withdrawn, unco-operative, etc.]?'

It is not always easy to be totally precise, but the following examples of a rewritten description of a child's behaviour may act as a guide.

Original Description

'Ann is a disruptive influence in class. She finds it difficult to concentrate and is disorganised. She seems to live in a world of her own and she is not popular with the other members of the class.'

Rewritten Description

'Ann often disrupts the class in that:

(a) She gets up from her place and walks around, often on the pretence of 'borrowing' something.

(b) She only works for short periods of time and then either fidgets

with her ruler or pen or prevents those children near her from working by talking to them.
(c) She makes noises, e.g. as an aeroplane or car, during writing times.

Ann often comes to class without the necessary equipment, e.g. pen, ruler, books or PE kit. The other pupils in the class often shun her by refusing to include her in either their group work or games. There has been no physical or verbal conflict between Ann and the other pupils.'

The difference between the two descriptions is quite clear. The first does not give any clear indication of what the exact problem is, only a vague, imprecise or 'woolly' outline. The second provides an excellent starting point for tackling the problem because we know what is actually happening within the classroom.

Summary

In order to adopt a positive behaviour management approach, the following questions provide a useful starting point:

(1) What exactly does the pupil do that causes concern?
(2) Can you list the behaviours?
(3) How often does each behaviour occur?
(4) When do each of the behaviours most commonly occur?
(5) In what setting does each behaviour occur?
(6) What consequences follow the behaviour?

Questions 1 and 2 could now be answered, bearing in mind the suggestions that have been made in this chapter.

It should now be possible to complete box 1 of the assessment chart. An example of a completed box 1 is shown at the beginning of Chapter 4. Question 3 enquires about the magnitude of the behaviours. The only way of determining this is through observation and accurate measurement and it is to these that we turn in the next chapter. Questions 4, 5 and 6 are the subjects of subsequent chapters.

Study Questions

(1) Why is it best to avoid labels such as 'maladjusted' and 'withdrawn'?

(2) What objections are there to using a 'medical model' of behaviour?

(3) What is the essential feature of a good description of behaviour?

(4) Which of these verbs would you reject when making an objective description of behaviour: says, understands, writes, resents, appreciates, cries, shouts?

(5) Which of the following statements would you describe as 'vague'?

(a) Carol's teacher gives her lots and lots of encouragement.

(b) Brian arrives to lessons within two minutes of the bell sounding with the other pupils.

(c) Sally sat at the front of the class and listened to the story with interest.

(d) Mrs Davis stimulated the group with a piece of classical music and they then wrote a piece of creative writing.

(e) From 10.00 a.m. to 1.15 a.m. John read aloud to the teacher.

(f) Kathy appreciated the way the teacher responded to her when she was upset.

(g) Keith is a maladjusted, acting-out adolescent.

(h) Amanda writes for about five minutes and then walks across the class to talk to her friends.

Answers to Study Questions

(4) You should have rejected 'understands', 'resents' and 'appreciates'. 'Says', 'writes', 'cries' and 'shouts' are actions we can *observe*.

(5)(a) Vague: 'lots and lots' is very unspecific. What is meant by encouragement?

(b) Well defined: we can see this happening and time it if desired, i.e. a criterion could be obtained.

(c) Vague: the words 'listen' and 'interest' are open to interpretation. We are not capable of knowing what is happening inside Sally's head.

(d) Vague: neither the verb 'stimulated' nor the adjective 'creative' are clear. Further definition is necessary.

(e) Well defined: we could see John reading aloud to the teacher.

(f) Vague: 'appreciates' and 'responds' are too imprecise. They do not tell us what the pupil or teacher actually does.

(g) Vague: 'maladjusted' and 'acting-out' are not precise. They give us no indication of what Keith actually does that leads us to make the statement.

(h) Well defined: it is quite clear what Amanda does.

4 OBSERVING AND MEASURING BEHAVIOUR

Figure 4.1: Assessment Chart. Observing and Measuring Behaviour

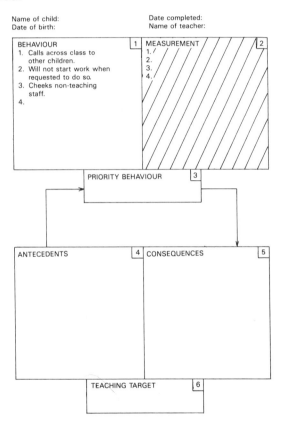

Aims

This chapter looks at the different strategies that are available to teachers for making accurate observations and measurements of behaviour. They allow us to quantify the descriptions that have been made of the behaviours. After reading this section you will be able to complete the 'measurement' box (No. 2) of the assessment chart (Figure 4.1).

Observing

Systematic observation and recording of a child's behaviour is an essential step in deciding on a programme for changing his behaviour. There are a number of reasons for this.

(a) It identifies more precisely the behaviours that are to be changed. For example, 'John hits other children' may become 'John hits Paul, Jane or Jason, on average twice a day during playtimes.'

(b) It modifies our preconception of the pupil. A child may be viewed as an 'attention seeker' because he constantly wants his work marked. Measuring this behaviour may reveal that, in fact, he does not request this any more frequently than do several other children in the class who are not regarded as 'attention seekers'. Hence, the measurement may lead us to redefine the problem by pointing out discrepancies between what is thought to be happening and what is *actually* occurring. Alternatively, the measurement may support the original perception of the problem.

(c) In situations where there is more than one behaviour which causes concern, measuring the frequency or duration of occurrence will allow us to form an order of priorities for change based on hard evidence rather than on impressions.

(d) It is almost impossible to recall accurately how often, where and when a pupil behaved in such a way without considering detailed observation records.

(e) Having established how often a pupil is behaving in a particular way before an intervention programme is begun, we can use this information (or baseline as it is called) to compare with his behaviour after our intervention. This allows us to evaluate the success (or otherwise) of our intervention — or at least to see if it is moving in the right direction.

(f) It may reveal that there is a pattern to the behaviour which in itself could suggest an intervention programme.

Measurement

Within the classroom there are a number of useful objective methods for selective observation and measuring of behaviour that may be used. The two most common forms of measurement are:

(a) *Event observation* — how often something happens over a period of time, i.e. *frequency* (e.g. how many times a pupil shouts out in a lesson).

(b) *Time observation* — how long a behaviour or event lasts during a period of observation, i.e. *duration* (e.g. how long a pupil remains 'on-task' or how much time he spends looking out of the window).

Measuring behaviour is not necessarily a complex or time-consuming task. The key to simplified recording is in limiting the number of behaviours to be observed and in describing them accurately so that they are easily identified.

Event Observation

This method (also known as frequency recording or tally method) is designed to give a measure of how frequently a behaviour or a range of behaviours occurs in specified settings, if it is the frequency of a behaviour which is giving rise to concern. The basis of the method is extremely simple. The behaviour is counted (tallied) each time it occurs in a specified period of time, for example:

Behaviour: Shouting out. Lesson: Topic work.
Length of observation: 30 minutes

꜔꜔꜔꜖ 1111   Total = 9

At the end of the period we can calculate the frequency of that behaviour by dividing the number of incidents by the length of the period. Hence:

$$\frac{\text{Number}}{\text{Time (in hours)}} = \frac{9}{0.5} = 18 \text{ per hour}$$

The particular unit you choose is not important: you may wish to record the frequency rate per minute, hour, day or week. It will depend on the frequency of the behaviour. For something that happens about twice a day a rate per minute is clearly inappropriate.

By expressing the behaviour in this way, you can compare different observation periods with each other: they do not have to be the same length of time. For example:

	Rate per hour
Day 1: 10 incidents in 30 minutes	20
Day 2: 22 incidents in 1 hour	22
Day 3: 5 incidents in 15 minutes	20
Day 4: 18 incidents in 1 hour	18
	Average = 20

Suitable Applications. Behaviours that are of short duration (leaving seat, punching, shouting out, throwing things, coming out to teacher's desk, etc.) and which occur fairly frequently can be recorded by this method.

For behaviours whose occurrence is unlikely to be missed by the teacher, e.g. shouts out to the teacher, coming to the teacher for help, bursting into tears, fighting in class, etc., it is quite straightforward for the teacher to record these herself. This can also be done for behaviours that leave a permanent record, e.g. a number of problems attempted in maths.

For some behaviours such as nudging, poking, interfering with others' work, etc., it can be difficult for a teacher to obtain frequency counts while at the same time attending to the needs of the whole class. This is also true if the frequency of more than one behaviour is required, unless they are very easily noticed. For these reasons, recording may need to be carried out by an observer who sits in an unobtrusive position in the classroom. In our experience we have known this role to be taken on by headteachers, supernumerary teachers, ancillary helpers, social workers, psychologists, etc. However, if a baseline of more than one behaviour is required, this can be achieved by recording only one behaviour at a time and then repeating the process for the other(s).

Limitations. Event observation has certain limitations:

(a) It is unsuitable for behaviours that occur at such high frequencies that it is impractical to record each incident individually, e.g. pencil tapping, rocking, etc.
(b) It is unsuitable for behaviours where duration is the important factor, e.g. time spent not working.
(c) It has the disadvantage that if a number of different behaviours are to be recorded, then a separate observer may be required. This can be overcome by recording the behaviours separately.

Advantages. Event observation has a number of important advantages, which make it a particularly useful method for classroom use:

(a) It is easy to use in a classroom setting as it does not require any sophisticated equipment.
(b) It does not interfere with classroom activities.
(c) It can be used with a wide range of behaviours.
(d) It focuses attention on naturally occurring 'chunks' of behaviour.
(e) It can produce records of behaviour over quite long time spans.

Guidelines for using event observation.

(1) Clearly identify and define the behaviour to be observed. With younger children this will usually be carried out by the child's teacher and may require the selection of one behaviour from among a number displayed in order for the recording to be easily carried out in the classroom situation. It is advisable to select a behaviour which is judged to be most amenable to change as it is important for both the teacher and the child to experience success when, later on, an intervention programme is put into effect. However, if a separate observer is available, it may be better to make a record of a number of the behaviours. This would allow the final choice of the target to be delayed until after the measurement — a preferred situation. In the case of older pupils, where a number of teachers are involved in the teaching, a group meeting should be arranged at which agreement can be reached on which behaviours are to be recorded.

(2) Know enough about the behaviour/s so that it can be decided when and where to make the observations and for what length of time they are to be made. For some infrequent behaviours it may be possible and desirable to make the recordings over a whole day or a whole week. For other, more frequently occurring behaviour (e.g. calling out), recording during a lesson or part of a lesson per day over the period of, say, one week may be sufficient.

(3) Decide how the behaviour is to be recorded. If a record sheet is to be employed, ensure that it is simple and easy to use.

(4) Sometimes it is inconvenient to tick a record sheet, and in these circumstances there are other methods that can be used for keeping a cumulative tally, e.g. knitting row counter, golf counter, shopper's counter, abacus or even moving counters from one pocket to another.

(5) If the behaviours are to be observed by more than one person at different times, then it is essential that all members of the recording team are quite clear as to the exact definition of the behaviours to be recorded.

(6) After the observations have been carried out for the period of time

decided upon, count up the incidents and calculate the rate per minute/hour/day as appropriate.

(7) Plot the results using a block or line graph so that you have a clearly established baseline against which to compare the behaviour/s after a period of intervention. See page 36 for an example of this.

Time Observation

If it is the duration of a behaviour which is of concern, then there are a number of different methods which may be employed to measure this. Two of the methods most likely to be employed in the classroom are dealt with here. Both strategies are a form of sampling in that the first, which we call *interval sampling*, consists of observing the child *continuously for a prearranged short time interval* whereas the second method, which we call *time sampling*, consists of observing the child at *prearranged moments in time*. It has been shown that the agreement between the methods where only a relatively small proportion of time is spent observing and constant observation is very high indeed. The great advantage is the time saved. For example, if, when using a time sampling method, twenty observations are made on a pupil during the course of a 40-minute period, this may occupy only one or two minutes of teacher time in total. This is a considerable saving on continuous observation and the results are likely to be just as accurate.

Interval Sampling. A typical use of interval sampling might be where the problem is inattention to the task in hand. This is often referred to as 'off-task' behaviour. Perhaps the teacher is concerned that in maths lessons the pupil produces insufficient work and appears to spend a great deal of time fiddling with things not relevant to the task or trying to attract the attention of other pupils. A decision is made to observe the pupil over the period of a week for a total time of 15 minutes each day during maths lessons. It is further decided that in order to establish a representative profile of behaviour the 15-minute observation interval should be divided into three 5-minute blocks. One could be at the start of the lesson, one in the middle and the third at the end. Each 5-minute block is futher divided into 1-minute sections and the pupil is observed throughout the whole of each 5-minute period. At the end of each 1-minute section, you record which of the behaviours occurred — fiddling (F) or attracting attention (A). If neither occurred, then the section is left blank. This will provide a measure of the proportion of time spent on task and the proportion spent in the two distracting activities. If the measurements are averaged over a period of one week, the results will be an accurate measure.

The following are suggested.

Guidelines for Using Interval Sampling

(1) Clearly define behaviour/s to be observed: frequently occurring behaviours that last for at least a few seconds are most appropriate, e.g. staring out of window, whining, thumb sucking, fidgeting, etc.

(2) Decide whether one or more behaviours are to be observed. Choose an easy code for these.

(3) Decide on the amount of time to be observed each day, whether this is to consist of one block or a number of subdivisions and when the observations are to take place. Within each time block decide on the length of the observation sections. These may be as short as 10 seconds or up to a minute in length. Thus a 5-minute time block could consist of ten 30-second intervals or five 1-minute intervals. There might be three or four (or any other number) such blocks within a day or week. Any appropriate combination may be employed.

(4) Decide on the form of the record sheet and how the data are to be recorded. Keep it simple and easy to use.

(5) Observe only during the prearranged set periods and record only what is observed during the time interval.

(6) At the end of the observation periods calculate the proportion — or the percentage if you prefer this — of the time that the child spent on the behaviours recorded.

(7) Plot the results on a bar graph or a line graph so that you have a clearly established baseline against which to compare the behaviour/s after a period of intervention.

Time Sampling. Although interval sampling has much to commend it, it will not have escaped your notice that it would be extremely difficult for the classteacher to carry it out unaided, and a separate observer is invariably required. This is not so with time sampling, which can be carried out easily by an unaided teacher.

This method is designed to give a measure of what proportion of time is spent by the child behaving in a particular way, e.g. what proportion of time does James spend staring out of the window? Observations of the child's behaviour are made at regular and prearranged intervals (i.e. sampling the behaviour). It might be decided to observe the child every 5 minutes or every 10 minutes. The child is observed at that time and it is recorded whether or not he is engaged *at that moment* in the behaviour which is being measured. For example:

Behaviour: Staring out of window (tick if observed)
Lesson: Maths   Observation interval: 5 minutes
Total time: 50 minutes

5	10	15	20	25	30	35	40	45	50
√	x	x	√	√	√	x	x	√	√

At the end of the period we can calculate what proportion of time is spent in the behaviour.

i.e. Proportion of time spent $= \dfrac{\text{No. of times occurring}}{\text{No. of times observed}}$

e.g. Proportion of time spent staring out of window $= \frac{6}{10} = 0.6$
(or as a percentage 60%)

You will need some form of reminder for the observation times — a wall clock, kitchen timer, interval timer, even an egg timer. A recording sheet will be needed which, if only one behaviour is being recorded, may be squared paper. Simply insert a tick if the behaviour is observed and a cross if it is not.

If more than one behaviour is being recorded, then a form of recording sheet is required showing the categories of behaviour to be recorded. Then all the teacher needs to do is place a check mark against any behaviour that is occurring at the time of the observation.

An example is shown in Figure 4.2. In this case two behaviours were being observed. It was decided to observe the child every 5 minutes during an observation period of 50 minutes each morning and each afternoon. This was done on four consecutive days. The teacher ticked the appropriate box if either behaviour was observed at the specified time and crossed both boxes through if neither was observed.

In this way a series of observations may be made at different times of the day during the course of, perhaps, one week. By this means a profile of behaviour is built up which will fairly accurately reflect the typical behaviour of the pupil.

Advantages of Time Sampling
   (a) Observations can be made relatively easily during the course of the whole day (time sampling).
   (b) The methods adopted may be extremely simple or highly sophisticated, according to the availability of trained staff and the types of behaviour to be observed.

Figure 4.2: Example of Time Sampling

Name: Observer:

Behaviours observed: A — Staring out of window
                     B — Being out of work base

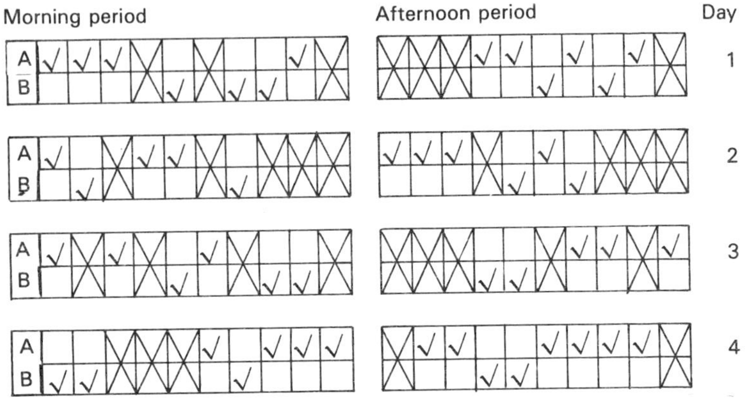

(c) More than one category of behaviour can be recorded simultaneously.

(d) Accurate estimates of behaviour are possible without the need for lengthy periods of continuous observation.

We suggest the following guidelines for using time sampling.

(1) Clearly define the behaviours to be observed: fairly frequently occurring behaviours that last at least for a few seconds are most appropriate. It is not suitable for brief behaviours (e.g. hitting and calling out) as it is unlikely that their incidence would coincide with an observation, thus giving a false measurement.

(2) Decide whether one or more behaviours are to be observed. Decide on the period of time for measurement and how frequently observations will be made during that period of time, e.g. a period of one hour's measurement and observations at 5-minute intervals during that time.

(3) Decide on the form of the record sheet and how the data are to be recorded. Time sampling will usually only require space for ticks or letters if more than one behaviour is being recorded.

(4) Decide on the form of the data. Will the check marks or time intervals

Name: Jamie
Behaviours:
Crying
Chewing teddy bear
Rocking
None of these observed
Observation: 50 minutes per day, 5-minute intervals, for 1 week

Age 4
Code
C
T
R
N

1st period of day

	5	10	15	20	25	30	35	40	45	50
Day 1	N	T	T	RT	N	N	N	N	RT	RT
Day 2	C	C	N	T	T	RT	RT	RT	N	N
Day 3	R	R	CR	N	N	N	N	C	C	CR
Day 4	C	T	T	T	CR	CR	N	N	N	N
Day 5	N	N	N	N	N	T	T	T	T	N

Proportion of time spent:

Crying $= \frac{9}{50} = 18\%$

Chewing teddy bear $= \frac{17}{50} = 34\%$

Rocking $= \frac{12}{50} = 24\%$

refer to 'on-task' or 'off-task' behaviour or will they refer to the presence or absence of a particular behaviour?

(5) Decide on the form of the signal which will remind you to take the observation.

(6) Observe only during the prearranged set periods and record only what is taking place at the time of the signal. Ignore what the child does just before or just after the signal.

(7) At the end of the observation periods calculate the proportion — or the percentage if you prefer this — of the time that the child spent on the behaviour recorded.

(8) Plot the results on a bar graph or line graph so that you have a clearly established baseline against which to compare the behaviour/s after a period of intervention.

An example of time sampling with more than one behaviour being recorded is shown above.

Other Methods

There are two other relevant methods which are worth noting at this stage.

Proportion Count

As the name implies, this recording technique is used when it is desired to record the proportion of times that a behaviour occurs related to the number of times it *could have* occurred. For example, you might express the number of times a child carries out an instruction as a proportion of the number of times instructions were given.

A proportion count is needed here as a child who complies with four out of four instructions is clearly different from one who complies with four out of sixteen (100 per cent as against 25 per cent). It is necessary simply to record as a tick or a cross the outcome of each occasion that the behaviour could occur. The percentage can then be calculated by:

$$\frac{\text{Number of ticks}}{\text{Total number of occasions}} \times 100$$

Appropriate Applications. This should be used only with behaviours that occur in clear circumstances where the teacher will not fail to observe them, e.g. complying with requests, waiting to be asked for an answer, number of sums correct out of the number attempted, etc.

Cumulative Timing

This method is used where the main interest is in the length of time that a behaviour lasts; for example, how much time a child spends working during a lesson, or how long it takes him to begin working at the start of a lesson. In the case of a single behaviour (e.g. starting work), it is simply a question of starting to time with a stopwatch at the beginning of the behaviour, stopping at the end and noting the result. In the case of an intermittent behaviour (e.g. working), you should use a cumulative stopwatch. Start the watch when he begins working; stop it when he stops working; start it again when he starts. Let the watch run only when he is working. At the end of the observation you will have a total of the time spent engaged in the observed behaviour.

Cumulative timing is usually difficult to apply in the classroom without an independent observer.

Observations of Whole Classes

Measuring procedures can also be used to observe the behaviour of groups or whole classes of children.

Time Sampling

Total class observation may be appropriate if the classteacher wants to change the behaviour of the group as a whole, e.g. the number of children queuing at her desk. Using time sampling, the number of children in the queue would be counted at the observation times and the average number found. The class could then be set targets to reduce this.

Event Sampling

Wherever the frequency of occurrence of a behaviour needs to be recorded, a frequency count involving the whole group or class can be used, e.g. numbers of pupils calling out in class, total number of homework assignments handed in on time.

Recording is simple with the help of a class list. Place a mark against the name of each pupil who shows the behaviour during each period of observation.

Cumulative Timing

Such a total may be appropriate if you wish to change a class behaviour in which children take part. For example, reducing time taken to settle down to work at start of lesson, shortening time taken to line up quietly before assembly.

Using a stopwatch, record time taken from the end of instructions given by the teacher to when the last pupil is no longer engaging in the observed behaviour.

Pupil Self-charting

With older pupils it may be possible to teach children to observe and record their own behaviour. This is known as self-charting or self-monitoring. The pupil records the number of times that he engages in the specified behaviour, such as shouting out in class. One simple method would be for the child to make a mark on a card 'every time you call out without permission'.

Initially, simultaneous self-monitoring and teacher monitoring may be needed to establish reliability and provide a daily point of contact for the discussion of discrepancies.

Self-charting provides the pupil with immediate feedback, encourages the child to accept responsibility for his own behaviour and frees the teacher of the need to observe and record pupil behaviour.

It must be said that this form of self-monitoring will *not* give baseline data for the behaviour. As the pupil is recording his own behaviour, this will in turn affect the frequency of that behaviour. Self-monitoring of behaviour can be a very effective form of intervention for some children. See Chapter 13.

Choosing a Method of Measurement

If you are in any doubt about the correct method to use, then by carefully working through the flow chart in Figure 4.3 you will be directed to the appropriate technique for the given behaviour. Note that if the suggested method is time observation, you may select time sampling or interval sampling depending on which is most convenient for you.

Charting the Results

Once you have obtained the measurements, you may wish to chart them on a graph to give visual representation. Sometimes this helps to clarify the situation in terms of patterns or trends. The graphs should be simple and easy to use. For many purposes a bar chart is perfectly adequate (see Figure 4.4).

Charting is useful when you remeasure the behaviour after intervention, as this helps to show any trends more closely. For example, Figure 4.5 shows the baseline and the evaluation of a programme designed to increase the proportion of time spent working. Days 1–6 represent the baseline and days 12–16 the evaluation.

These data could alternatively be plotted in a conventional manner, as in Figure 4.6. From this it can clearly be seen that there is a significant improvement and that progress is being maintained. Obviously the intervention programme should be continued.

Study Questions

(1) For what reasons is it important to carry out systematic observations?

Figure 4.3: Choosing a Method of Measurement

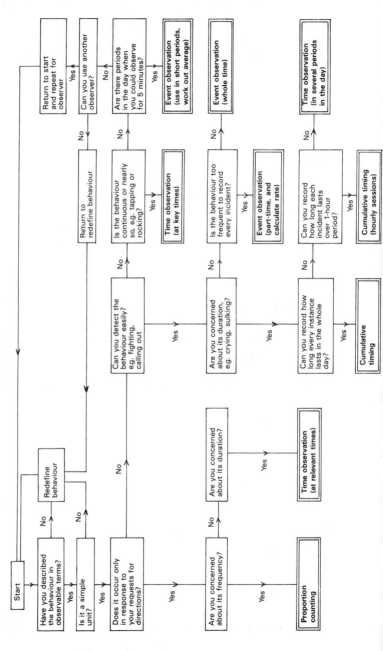

Figure 4.4: An Example Bar Chart

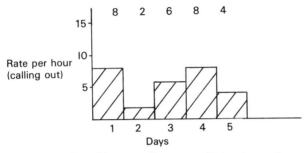

Figure 4.5: Bar Chart to Compare Behaviour after Intervention

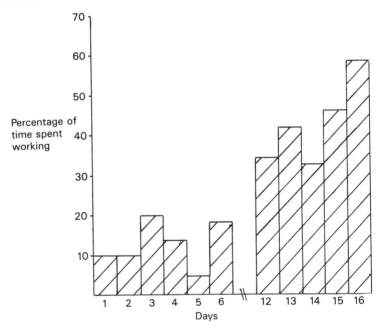

(2) What are the two main methods of measuring behaviour?
(3) Which method of measurement might you use with the following behaviours?

    (a) interrupting teacher;
    (b) kicking;
    (c) crying;

Figure 4.6: Graph to Compare Behaviour after Intervention

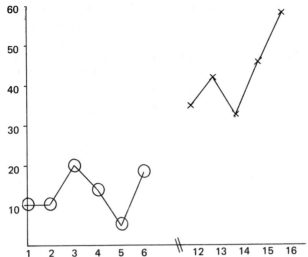

(d) tapping ruler;
(e) refusing to carry out instructions;
(f) arriving late to lessons;
(g) making whining noises;
(h) whole class slow to settle down to work.

(4) Why is it useful to convert data into rates?
(5) What is a baseline?

Answers to Study Question 3

(a) Event observation. All you need here is a simple tally of the number of occasions it occurs. It is an easy behaviour to count as you are very unlikely to miss it.

(b) Event observation again. It is presumably the frequency of this behaviour that is the concern. The behaviour is likely to be very brief and thus sampling would miss the great number of occurrences.

(c) Not a clear answer here. Either event or time observation might be appropriate. The choice would depend on whether you were more concerned about the frequency of the crying or the length of time each incident lasted. The individual situation would

determine your priorities.
(d) Time observation. Quite likely the choice would be time sampling for ease of use in the classroom as you are probably interested in the proportion of time spent in this activity.
(e) Proportion count. It is relatively easy to record the number of instructions given and the number that were refused, and then to work out the proportion as an accurate measure of the behaviour.
(f) A variety of choices here. It depends whether you are concerned about the number of occasions on which this happens or the amount by which the pupil is late. Again the choice will be between event observation and time observation, depending on the individual situation. However, a further choice may exist. For an older pupil you may ask him to record his own performance as part of a self-monitoring programme.
(g) Again, it depends on the individual situation. If the noises are produced for a lengthy period of time, then time sampling would be appropriate. If they are of short duration, then event observation would be easier.
(h) Cumulative timing. Although usually a demanding technique for a classteacher to employ with an individual, it is quite straightforward to use with a whole-class behaviour such as this.

5 DECIDING ON PRIORITIES

Figure 5.1: Assessment Chart. Choosing a Priority Behaviour

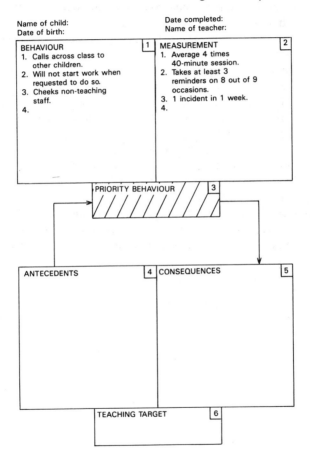

Aims

This section is designed to facilitate the choice of which behaviour(s) should become the target for change. After reading this section you will be able to complete the 'priority behaviour' box (No. 3) of the assessment chart (Figure 5.1).

Choosing a Priority Behaviour

By the time this stage has been reached, a considerable amount of data will have been collected on the behaviour of the pupil in question. His behaviour will have been described in precise terms and data collected concerning either its frequency or duration.

It is not unusual to have found that those behaviours which had been considered most frequent prior to the making of structured observations do not, in fact, occur all that often. They may have seemed to happen more frequently because they were of a type that caused the greatest concern, such as physical attacks on other pupils. It is also the case that the most serious behaviours may occur because a more frequently occurring but less serious behaviour provides the opportunity for it. Typically, a child who punches or prods another child does so when he has left his place but he leaves his place much more often than he assaults other pupils. You must, therefore, be prepared to review your previous priority of concern in the light of the measurements that you have obtained.

When confronted with a list of behaviours and the measurements obtained for them, you may be tempted to decide that all these must be tackled. However, a moment's consideration will reveal that such a project would not only be unrealistic but would also have as its target the production of a perfect child! Your targets must be realistic and attainable for the child. They must also be compatible with the other children's behaviour in that he should not be asked to behave in a way that is superior to the class average.

It is perhaps a cliché but the notion that success breeds success is nowhere truer than in the field of behavioural change. Therefore, if you are dealing with the first intervention, this should tackle a behaviour that is amenable to change, even if this is not the most serious problem. If this is successful, then both you and the pupil will be more motivated to continue with the more difficult problems.

It is crucial to understand that the first aim must be to achieve success both for the pupil and for the teacher. We want to see improvement and thus to be able to be genuinely positive in our approach to the child. We want the pupil to be pleased that we are pleased. We want him to learn, perhaps for the first time, that acceptable behaviour is noticed and rewarded.

For these reasons it is wise to choose as the priority behaviour one which is likely to be changed successfully. It is also necessary to choose only one behaviour and to concentrate upon this.

In our cumulative example it will be noted that 'Will not start work when requested' has been chosen as the priority behaviour (see Figure 6.1). The logic of this is self-evident. If the child is working, then the likelihood of his calling out is much lessened. Cheeking non-teaching staff once a week is undesirable but concentrating upon this is unlikely to bring about any changes in the other areas of behaviour which occur much more frequently.

Improvements in the child's willingness to start work are going to bring about the possibility of regular expressions of approval from the teacher, which in turn will develop a positive pupil/teacher relationship which *may* make the child more amenable to a further subsequent suggestion that he should not cheek non-teaching staff.

Particularly with older children, it is desirable, bordering on essential, to discuss the choice of priority with the child. There is a higher likelihood of success if the child is a co-operative and actively participating partner in the intervention rather than simply 'having things done to him'. Any time spent on this activity is time well spent. All too often in the past, some behaviour modification programmes have had limited success or the problems have returned after the programme has been discontinued. Frequently, the reason for this has been that although everyone associated with the pupil — parents, teachers, etc. — have recognised the need for change and agreed on its direction, the pupil has not. This may simply be due to his not recognising that some behaviours are inappropriate in general terms, for, as far as he is concerned, they may be very appropriate or indeed important to him. It is only by negotiation and discussion that the need for change can be perceived and agreed. The aim of any behaviour management programme must be for the pupil to recognise the need for change, agree on its direction, be a willing participant, and perceive that the situation would be improved by the changes. Behavioural change without these conditions tends towards being imposed change from outside the pupil, with the likelihood that the problems may reappear after the intervention is withdrawn. It also raises certain important ethical questions about the rights of the individual regarding such change. The most successful behavioural change is that which results in a cognitive change on the part of the pupil. That is to say that the changes are perceived by him as being beneficial and are thus more likely to be consolidated as part of his everyday behaviour. The changes are then maintained by the individual himself and his social interactions with others and not by another person acting as a control. This, quite obviously, is to be preferred as a general ethical model where individuals maintain responsibility and control over their own lives and behaviour.

Summary of Guidelines in Choosing the Priority Behaviour

(1) Choose one behaviour only.
(2) Choose one with which you are likely to succeed.
(3) Discuss and negotiate the choice with the pupil.
(4) When entering this on the assessment chart, word the behaviour in such a way that it expresses a behaviour that you wish to reduce in either frequency or duration.

Study Questions

(1) Why should you use only one priority behaviour at a time?
(2) What are some of the important criteria to be observed when choosing a priority behaviour?

6   ENVIRONMENT AND BEHAVIOUR — AN ABC

Figure 6.1: Assessment Chart. Environment and Behaviour

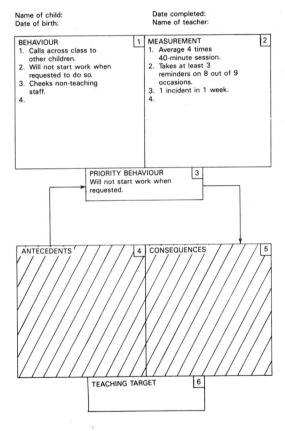

Aims

So far attention has been focused on the behaviours produced by the child. In this chapter attention is given to the environment in which the behaviour occurs, and in particular to events that precede and follow the incidence of that behaviour. After reading this section it will be possible to complete the 'antecedents' and 'consequences' boxes (Nos 4 and 5) of the assessment chart (Figure 6.1).

The Environment and Behaviour

In previous chapters the focus of attention has been upon the behaviours produced by the child. Apart from noting the time of day or the lesson in progress, little attention was paid to the environment in which the behaviour occurred. This is by no means because the importance of this is being minimised but only because the actual behaviours provide a logical starting point in the analysis.

It is central to the positive behaviour management approach that *behaviour does not occur randomly or accidentally*. A full understanding of what promotes a behaviour and, the behaviour having been promoted, maintains it can only be acquired by looking away from the behaviour itself to the environment, to the events that preceded the behaviour and those that follow it.

It has been stated earlier that behaviour does not occur in a random manner. It could be argued that every action that is taken by a living organism is informed by the experiences to which it has been subjected in the past. This is not to say that people only act in ways that are laid down by past experiences because that would imply that there is no place for independent thought or action. However, the fact that people choose or do not choose to produce particular ways of behaving is itself the result of what has happened in the past. It is necessary to *learn* to be a conformist or to be a revolutionary, and what is more to *learn* to choose to be one or the other at any particular time.

If we choose to smile at a stranger before asking directions in a strange town, it is because we have learnt that a smile is a way of assuring our fellow human beings that our approach is friendly and that they do not need to fear us. If, however, we find that our smile is greeted with a scowl or even a stream of bad language, this would have certain effects upon the way in which we approach strangers in future. We might investigate the reason for our greeting being returned in this atypical way. Is the behaviour peculiar to the particular individual we approached, or is this the usual way the inhabitants of this town behave? In other words we would seek, if we were of an analytical frame of mind, to shift the focus of attention away from the actual behaviour itself and concentrate on the factors that conspired to bring it about. This would also mean that we would not be reacting to the behaviour itself, i.e. the scowl or the invective, but to the environment in which it occurred. This shift of emphasis is more positive in terms of deciding how to avoid or handle such events in the future.

An example will serve to illustrate this analytical approach as applied to the learning of appropriate behaviours. The bell for the end of lunch-time has sounded. Joanne walks into the classroom, collects a worksheet, goes to her place and starts to work. Following the suggestions given in earlier sections we can state Joanne's behaviour in precise terms:

> *Observed behaviour:* Joanne enters the room, helps herself to a worksheet, walks to her place, sits down and commences work.

She does all these things without appearing to have received any instructions to do so, yet it is clear that this is not random behaviour. What has happened is that Joanne has received a considerable number of environmental cues which have directed her to act in this way. Among these might be the sight of other children walking to the classroom following the signal given by the bell. The worksheets are piled in their customary place, a set of instructions might be written on the blackboard and, most importantly, similar sequences of events have taken place many times before.

Joanne has responded to a number of environmental cues which may be called *antecedents* because they occurred before or existed in the environment before the behaviour takes place. This complex of antecedents combine to inform Joanne of the behaviour she should produce in the classroom setting. Some of these antecedents such as the customary arrangements in the classroom are quite tangible, others are less so. These could include Joanne's knowledge of the teacher, her attitude towards the subject taught and her own emotional and physical feeling at the time. This situation might be summarised as follows:

Example 1

Antecedents	Behaviour
(1) Bell rings.	
(2) Other pupils walk to the classroom.	
(3) Instructions written on blackboard.	Joanne comes into class-room, takes a worksheet,
(4) Worksheets available in usual place.	starts work.
(5) Teacher in classroom.	
(6) Science laboratory.	
(7) Feeling well.	

The antecedents present in a situation may not always produce such an acceptable result. The same analytical approach can be used to find out why this should be so. For instance, taking the last example and altering some of the antecedents, the following situation might well occur:

Example 2

Antecedents	Behaviour
(1) Bell rings.	
(2) Some children continue to talk in corridor.	
(3) Diagram from last period still on blackboard.	Joanne strolls into room and joins a group of children chatting by the window.
(4) Worksheets under the register and not easily visible.	
(5) Teacher in stockroom getting out apparatus.	
(6) Science laboratory.	
(7) Feeling well.	

Antecedents, then, are those aspects of the environment that provide cues about the behaviours to be produced *before* the behaviours occur. We now need to turn our attention to those events that occur *after* the behaviour has taken place. These are termed *consequences*. They are of the utmost importance because it is these events that will either increase or decrease the likelihood of the behaviour being repeated.

In our hypothetical example concerning the response to the smile given in a strange town, we already know that the consequence was a scowl or stream of bad language. A number of further consequences might follow this but it is fairly certain that at the very least the likelihood of a smile occurring again in similar circumstances would be reduced.

We are now in a position to carry our analysis of Joanne's behaviour one stage further to include the consequences.

Example 3

Antecedents	*Behaviour*	*Consequences*
(1) Bell rings.		
(2) Other pupils walk to the classroom.		

(3) Instructions written on blackboard.	Joanne enters classroom and starts work.	1. Verbal praise. 2. Help given to pupils working.
(4) Worksheets available in usual place.		
(5) Teacher in classroom.		
(6) Science laboratory.		
(7) Feeling well.		

Reinforcers and Punishers

Research has shown that consequences which closely follow a behaviour can either strengthen or weaken the likelihood of that behaviour being repeated. Those consequences that strengthen a behaviour and make it more likely to occur again in the future are known as *reinforcers*. Those consequences that weaken a behaviour, making it less likely to occur again, are called *punishers* or *punishing stimuli*.

Reinforcement is used to shape and strengthen desired target behaviour. Reinforcers commonly used in schools include praise, attention, good marks for work, access to privileges and special activities.

Punishment is used to reduce the frequency, duration or intensity of undesirable behaviour. Punishments commonly used in schools include verbal reprimands or criticism, bad marks for work, loss of privileges, detentions, etc.

Unfortunately, the relationship between reinforcement, punishment and behaviour in specific situations is not always crystal-clear at first sight.

Although the consequences that immediately follow a behaviour may be reinforcing and increase the likelihood that such behaviour will occur again, this may not always be what was intended. They may be applied by the teacher with a view to their having precisely the opposite effect to that obtained or they may be applied quite unknowingly.

A typical example of this is where a teacher responds to a behavioural tantrum by holding the child in a warm, soothing and comforting way. This is likely to be reinforcing (rewarding) to the child and make it more likely that tantrum behaviour will be repeated.

An example of an unknowingly applied punishment might be where a child, having taken great pains with a piece of work, shows it to the teacher who merely glances at it without comment. Here, the likelihood is that 'trying behaviour' is punished and 'non-trying' behaviour is reinforced. This is obviously a great problem for teachers who have to make many instant responses to a wide variety of behaviour in the pressurised environment of the classroom. However, some of the commonly occurring response errors can be avoided if teachers are more aware of these difficulties.

This can be further illustrated by returning to our theme example where Joanne has strolled into the room and has joined a group of children who are chatting.

Example 4

Antecedents	*Behaviour*	*Consequences*
(1) Bell rings.		
(2) Some children continue to talk in corridor.		
(3) Diagram from last period still on blackboard.	Joanne strolls into room and joins a group idly chatting.	Teacher arrives in classroom late and goes to Joanne and the other pupils who are out of their seats and helps them to get started.
(4) Worksheets under the register and not easily visible.		
(5) Teacher in stockroom getting out apparatus.		
(6) Science laboratory.		
(7) Feeling well.		

In this example the teacher has gone out of his way to pay attention to, and thus reinforce, the inappropriate behaviours produced by the children, thereby ensuring that such behaviours will occur more frequently. These unintended reinforcers are just as potent and effective as those that are intended but are undermining the teacher's management strategy.

Such sequences of events may be observed occurring regularly in schools, homes, supermarkets, playgrounds, etc. Children (and adults) produce unacceptable behaviours and are immediately rewarded (i.e. successfully reinforced), often by being given individual, undivided attention. All too often, acceptable behaviours go unnoticed or unrewarded.

Summary

Behaviours occur in a sequence of events, in fact an ABC: antecedents precede the behaviour and the child responds to these (i.e. behaves); consequences occur after behaviour, and influence future behaviour by making it either more or less likely to occur.

The direct implications of these are that behaviour can be taught or problem behaviours modified by manipulating the environment in which the child lives. Hence, if we have children who have behaviour or academic problems, it means that given the right approach and information, we can redesign the environment to help them learn more appropriate ways of behaving or working. It will be noticed that this is a *positive approach* in terms of *action*.

Looking at Antecedents and Consequences

On most occasions it will be a straightforward matter to determine the antecedents and consequences of a particular behaviour. Sometimes it may be rather more complicated. This would certainly be the case if the situation in question were that of a confrontation between a pupil and teacher which proceeded from a very low-level interaction to one where heated words were exchanged or a blow was thrown. The following list of questions should serve as a guide to obtain the necessary information. It should be noted that not all the questions will be relevant to all behaviours and all situations. This list is not intended to be exhaustive.

What was the pupil doing just before the incident?
What were the other pupils doing?
What were you doing?
In what task was the pupil engaged?
How competent is he at this task?
In what task were the other pupils engaged?
Were there any special circumstances?
What was the pupil seen to do?
What did the other pupils do?
What did you do?
When did it happen?
Where did it happen?
What action did you take as a result?
What did the pupil then do?

How did the pupil react to you and the other pupils?
What happened as a result of this incident?

An example of a simple breakdown of the ABC in the assessment phase is given below. The behaviour giving rise to concern is 'calling out'.

Antecedents

Not being asked to give the answer/comment himself.
Class discussion time.

Behaviour

John calls out comments to classteacher.

Consequences

Verbal reprimand from teacher ('Don't call out'). Smiles and approval for John from others in class.

Evaluation (Was the Intervention Successful?)

Stops that instant but repeats shortly afterwards.

You will note that a further section has been added, evaluation, i.e. what happened as a result of the handling of the situation. We need to examine openly and without bias whether the intervention chosen is appropriate and successful. Here the original handling — the verbal reprimand — was successful in the short term but did nothing to prevent the behaviour repeating itself.

Study Questions

(1) What is an antecedent?
(2) What is a consequence and what effect can it have on behaviour?
(3) Why is it important to identify unintended reinforcers?
(4) Read the following and then answer the question below:

Colin is a pupil in his first year at the local comprehensive. The scene is a maths lesson in the middle of the week. The class is working quietly under the supervision of Mr Wilson. There is a knock at the classroom door. It is the Deputy Head, Mrs Cliff.
   'Can I have a word please, Mr Wilson?'
   'Right, carry on quietly, Class 4'.

Mr Wilson leaves the class and goes into the corridor with Mrs Cliff. Mark, sitting directly behind Colin, leans forward and prods him with the tip of a pair of compasses. Colin turns round saying 'Pack it in, will you'. Undeterred, and much to the amusement of some of the others in the class who encourage him, Mark jabs Colin again. He turns round and repeats his last comment amid some laughter from others in the class. At this point Mr Wilson puts his head round the door saying 'A little less noise. I'm talking with Mrs Cliff'.

'Please, Sir . . .' starts Colin.

'Not now' replies Mr Wilson, returning to the corridor. A few moments later, Mark attempts one more jab, only to be stopped in the act by Colin turning round and holding his arm.

'Let go!' shouts Marks, wrenching his arm free and jabbing with the compass. Colin at this point hits Mark, timing it just as Mr Wilson re-enters the room.

'I wondered what the noise was before. I see now that it's you who can't behave yourself when I am out of the room. Colin, see me at the end of the lesson and you will then go to your Head of House.'

This is a stylised incident but one that contains some important examples of antecedents and consequences. What are the antecedents and consequences for the two key pieces of behaviour in this story?

(a) Mark jabs Colin for the second time.
(b) Colin hits Mark following his attempted third jab.

7 SELECTING A TEACHING TARGET

Figure 7.1: Assessment Chart. Selecting a Teaching Target

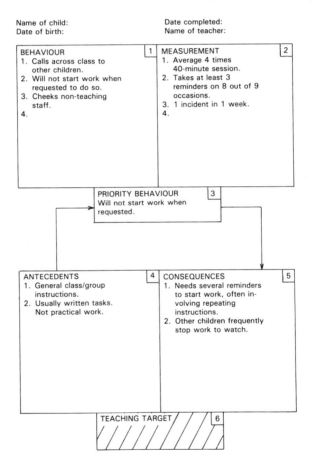

Aims

This section is concerned with selecting the target behaviour that is to be taught. After reading this section you will be able to complete the 'teaching target' box (No. 6) on the assessment chart (Figure 7.1).

Selecting a Teaching Target

The assessment phase of the positive behaviour management approach is now very nearly complete. In our worked example the behaviours giving rise to concern have been identified and observed and an accurate measurement of the incidence of each one has been obtained. Of the three behaviours observed, one has been found to occur only rarely whereas failing to start work when requested to do so is extremely consistent, i.e. on eight of nine occasions three reminders are required before work is commenced. Although this is a hypothetical example, it is very likely that were it to be an actual case, the main concern of the teacher before the objective measurements were made would have been the 'calling out' behaviour.

The choice of 'will not start work when requested' as the target behaviour rested on two factors. First, it represents the greatest influence running counter to the child's satisfactory academic progress, and secondly, it is a contributory factor to the 'calling out' behaviour. Simply, a child cannot be calling across the classroom to other members of the class if he is engaged in working.

Having selected the priority behaviour, the *teaching target* is quite simply the behaviour that the child is required to display instead of the unacceptable priority behaviour. For example, if the priority behaviour is 'pushing other children out of the way when forming a queue' then the teaching target could be 'joins a queue at the end and waits turn without fuss'.

Three important considerations should be borne in mind when choosing a teaching target.

(1) Choose a teaching target that is incompatible with the priority behaviour. That is to say, choose a teaching target such that the child cannot display both the priority behaviour and the teaching target *at the same time*. For example:

Priority behaviour	*Teaching target*
running around class	walking in class
staring out of window	writing in book
sitting on desk, working	sitting on chair, working
interrupts teacher	waits for teacher to stop talking
uses foul language	uses acceptable adjectives
scratches children	shares toys without fuss

(2) When choosing a teaching target, attempt to word it in such a way that an increase rather than a decrease in behaviour is required. This may seem an insignificant point but it is easier to teach a child *to do something* rather than *not to do it*. It is also easier for the child to learn to do something which is positive and can be seen to be happening rather than to learn not to do something which can then only be identified by its absence. To do something is relatively concrete whereas not to do something is an abstraction. Such a choice is also more in keeping with the positive approach we are emphasising. For example:

Undesirable teaching targets	*Positive teaching targets*
stop interrupting	put up hand
stop snatching from other children	say please and ask to borrow equipment
stop wetting in class	go to the toilet when necessary
stop chewing pencil	keep pencil in good condition
stop forgetting PE kit	come with PE kit

A little practice is all that is required in pairing the priority behaviour and teaching target in this way.

(3) Word the target in such a way that it is realistic for the pupil:

    (a) in relation to his present performance;
    (b) in relation to the performance of the other pupils in the class.

In other words don't ask him to make too large a step in his development or expect him to be an angel in comparison with his peers.

The assessment part of this book is now complete and the full assessment chart is shown in Figure 7.2. Steps 1, 2, 3 and 4 have been covered. In Part 3 of the book we shall deal with Steps 5 and 6, which are concerned with intervention.

Study Questions

(1) What is the relationship between the priority behaviour and the teaching target?
(2) What are the three important considerations that should be borne in mind when selecting a teaching target?
(3) Write down the names of five pupils whom you teach or have recently

Figure 7.2: Completed Assessment Chart

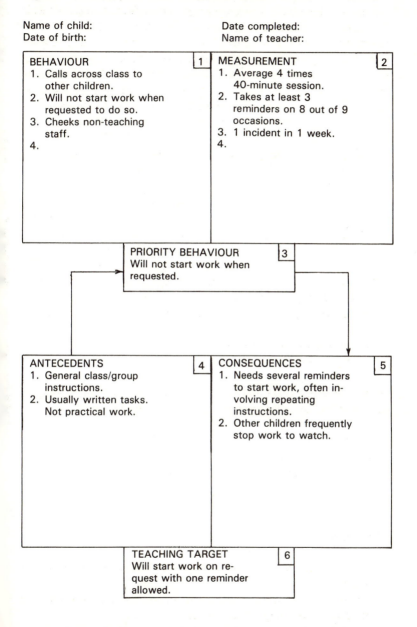

Name of child: Date completed:
Date of birth: Name of teacher:

BEHAVIOUR | 1 |
1. Calls across class to other children.
2. Will not start work when requested to do so.
3. Cheeks non-teaching staff.
4.

MEASUREMENT | 2 |
1. Average 4 times 40-minute session.
2. Takes at least 3 reminders on 8 out of 9 occasions.
3. 1 incident in 1 week.
4.

PRIORITY BEHAVIOUR | 3 |
Will not start work when requested.

ANTECEDENTS | 4 |
1. General class/group instructions.
2. Usually written tasks. Not practical work.

CONSEQUENCES | 5 |
1. Needs several reminders to start work, often involving repeating instructions.
2. Other children frequently stop work to watch.

TEACHING TARGET | 6 |
Will start work on request with one reminder allowed.

taught. For each pupil list one behaviour that you would like to change. Treat this list as if they were priority behaviours and now write a teaching target for each, bearing in mind the criteria given in this chapter.

PART 3:

INTERVENTION

8 STRATEGIES FOR PROMOTING BEHAVIOURAL CHANGE

Introduction

In Part 2 we examined a method of analysing in detail, behaviours and the environmental factors that serve to promote and maintain these behaviours. This ABC of behavioural analysis, which allows the accurate assessment to be carried out, also provides much of the information which is required to bring about change.

The strategies that we shall discuss in this section will have some things in common with traditional methods of behaviour management that have been used in education in the past. However, there will be many very important differences. The most important of these is the emphasis on a *truly positive approach*. All too often, educationists talk about creating a positive atmosphere in a class or school but resort to negatively framed rules or controls in their day-to-day management. Certainly most people's experience of school is of a situation where most rules (*if* they were made explicit!) are worded in the manner of the following examples: 'Don't run in the corridors', 'No leaving the room without permission', 'No talking unless called upon', etc.

Fortunately some schools are now much more aware of the negative effects of such rules and have translated them into positives. Small changes such as this can have quite large benefits.

The traditional approach also tends to concentrate on the behaviour produced and to try to bring about changes by corrective instructions such as: 'Get on with your work', 'Don't call out', 'Stop being silly', 'Stop talking', etc. The success of such an approach may be judged by the number of times that these instructions have to be repeated.

The positive behaviour management approach differs from the traditional approach because at least equal importance is accorded to the antecedents and consequences of the behaviour as to the behaviour itself. This is a great advantage to teachers, who are in a very powerful position because they have the major control over most antecedents and consequences and can therefore change them. There will always be some that will not be within the teacher's sphere of influence, but even here it is sometimes possible to bring about change indirectly.

The positive behaviour management approach is also a great advantage to the pupil. He is no longer a passive reactor to instructions and controls being exerted upon him. Rather he is an active participant in his own development. It is vital to view the approach in this way for, although the teacher is in a strong position, children have a large influence over their own behaviour. Without the child's participation as a full and valued partner, all that is likely to be achieved is control in certain situations. This only solves problems in the short term. With the child as partner, long-term cognitive change can be achieved which, with careful planning, may generalise to other situations.

Strategies for Promoting Behavioural Change

Teachers will be concerned with behaviours that are either not happening frequently enough or that are happening too often. These are referred to as behavioural deficits or behavioural excesses. The aim of a management programme would generally be to increase the frequency of the behavioural deficits and to reduce the behavioural excesses. Questions such as these are often asked:

'How can I get him to do "A"?'
'How can I get him to stop "B"?'

These are usually followed very closely by:

'Now that he is doing "A", how can I make sure this continues?'
'Now that he has stopped doing "B", how can I make sure it stays that way?'

Having analysed the various bits of the ABC puzzle through the assessment process, you should be in a good position to decide which variable (or variables) needs to be worked on in order to effect change. It may be the antecedents, including the background, or the consequences or some combination of both.

These changes may be quite significant or they may be quite minor. You should at this stage, if you have not already done so, check to see if a direct or informal solution is possible. For example, a direct request or command telling a child to stop picking his nose, explaining that others may find this offensive, may be sufficient. A child who is not getting enough sleep may be irritable or unable to concentrate. A discussion with parents over an earlier bedtime may be the solution to this problem.

Alterations in the routine of the class may effect change, e.g. giving a child increased responsibility — the poacher-turned-gamekeeper ploy. The informal role to bear in mind when reading the remainder of the book is: never use a more powerful intervention than is necessary. No sledgehammers cracking walnuts!

It is appropriate, at this stage, to repeat that behaviour management is a craft, a mixture of art and science. There is no one 'right solution' to all problems of a certain type. Equally there is no one 'right way' to arrive at a solution to a problem. Problems and solutions are as many and varied as the people who are part of them. This manual seeks to provide a framework on which to build. It is not intended to be followed slavishly. The methods and techniques discussed in Part 3 must be evaluated by the reader in the light of the circumstances and problems which are of concern. Some of them are more appropriate to younger children and others more to older pupils and adolescents. We trust that this is clear from the text. The final choice for intervention must lie with the teacher for only he or she knows the problem and its situation first hand.

Part 3 introduces the intervention chart, which is shown in Figure 8.1. This plays a similar role to that played by the assessment chart in Part 2. It co-ordinates the planning of an intervention strategy based on the data gathered in the assessment phase.

The following chapters in this part of the book will examine each of the ABC elements in turn. The aim is to determine how these can be manipulated in order to bring about behavioural change.

At this stage it may be useful to present a brief overview (which is certainly not all inclusive) of some of the strategies that will be discussed in depth subsequently.

Strategies for Changing Behaviour

Re-arranging Antecedents

   (a) Give clear instructions, making the rules explicit and reminding pupils of them. Provide behavioural rehearsal.

   (b) Give an early warning: lessen the impact of bad news by allowing the child to plan his remaining time or actions.

   (c) Give good news with bad: this pairing can reduce the side-effects associated with a reprimand.

   (d) Change your own behaviour: both verbal and non-verbal.

   (e) Change the setting: altering the physical environment or social setting is a positive way of preventing problem behaviours.

Figure 8.1: Intervention Chart

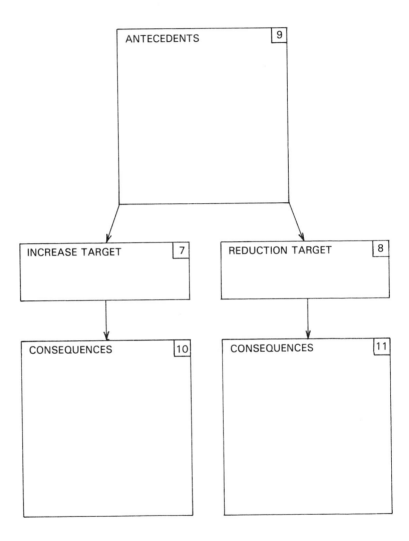

Removing temptation also falls into this category.

(f) Introduce a prompt: use non-verbal cues to signal appropriate and inappropriate behaviours.

Teaching Competing Behaviour

(a) Help the child learn a new skill or behaviour which is incompatible with the problem behaviour.

(b) Suggest the pupil uses an alternative behaviour in order to prevent the occurrence of the problem behaviour.

Changing the Consequences

(a) Selective attention: ignoring the behaviour (extinction).

(b) Positive reinforcement and reward of good behaviour.

(c) Sharing the responsibility for the situation: using contracting.

(d) Punishing unwanted behaviours.

(e) Using time out: removing a pupil from a difficult situation for a short period of time.

9 BEHAVIOUR TARGETS

Figure 9.1: Intervention Chart. Behaviour Targets

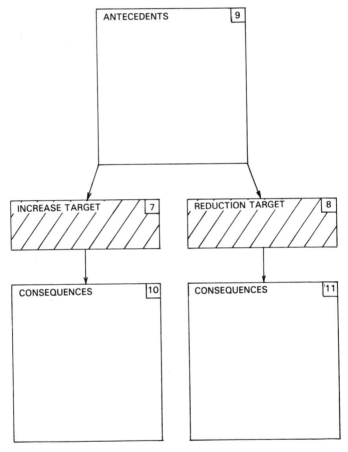

Aims

This section deals with specification of behaviour targets in a manner likely to lead to success. It also examines criteria for these targets. After reading this section you will be able to complete the reduction and increase target boxes (Nos 7 and 8) on the intervention chart (Figure 9.1).

Selection and Control of Behaviour Targets

By the time this stage is reached, there will already be available a list of behaviours that it is desirable either to increase or to eliminate. Baselines will have been obtained regarding intensity, duration or priority ranking of these behaviours.

If we consider the behaviours that it is desirable to eliminate, it would clearly be unrealistic to make the first target the cessation of all unsatisfactory behaviours. A choice will have been made from the behaviours, bearing in mind their priority ranking. Having made the choice of one behaviour on which to focus attention, it would still be unrealistic to make the first target the total elimination of this behaviour. It may be necessary to have intermediate targets on the way to the final target. For instance, if a child is fighting at break times on average eight times a week, it would almost certainly be expecting too much if we were to set the target at zero fights. Intermediate targets of four and then two and then zero may be more easily attainable goals for the child. It is important to remember that if a task appears too daunting for the child, then it is likely that he will not even try to reach it. The targets must be realistic, attainable and in line with the behaviour of the other children in the class.

Similarly, with regard to behaviours that it is desired to increase, it may often be unrealistic to expect the pupil to attain a level compatible with the remainder of the class in one step. A similar approach of using 'steps to target' should be used. For example, if the problem is that the child does not produce as much written work as the others in the class, although it is within his capabilities, then the targets expected of him should be increased gradually, say from five lines to ten lines to twenty lines, etc.

The choice of appropriate standards and the size of the steps designed to attain them are of crucial importance and merit further consideration.

Selecting Appropriate Standards

The standards expected should be those that are the norm for the class, group or school. Additionally they should be appropriate for the sex, age, ability and development of the child. In many cases teachers will have a good idea of 'what is reasonable'. However, it is very easy to fall into the trap of setting standards by what you think is happening rather than what is actually happening. This applies not only to your perception of what the remainder of the class are actually doing but also to what your target pupil is doing. One's awareness of a pupil's actions can be heightened because of earlier difficulties, and thus the instances of his behaviour have a greater effect than those of others in the class doing exactly the same thing. This can lead one to think that the problem is still a problem when in fact the pupil is no worse than the rest of the class. It might be argued that there still is a problem, but perhaps it is not the child's!

The answer is to record the behaviour of others in the class who are not perceived as a problem in order to arrive at a norm for the situation. This will than act as your target for the behaviour of the 'problem pupil'.

Deciding the Size of Steps

The size of the steps is difficult to specify too far in advance. There are no hard and fast rules for determining this. It is usually possible to specify the size of the first one or two but subsequent steps should be left flexible. Step size depends on:

(a) The child's entry skill, i.e. at what level was he performing at the start of the programme?
(b) How large is the gap between his performance and that of the rest of the group?
(c) How quickly did he manage the last step?

The trick is to arrive at a balance between having too many steps such that they are redundant and time-wasting and having too few such that the gap between them is too great for the pupil to achieve, resulting in his giving up.

If the child is old enough, then the setting of steps and the desired outcome should be discussed with him. Again, if the child is an active participant in the process, there is a much greater chance of success with the programme initially and in establishing change in the long term.

Teaching Competing Behaviour

It is vital that at least as much thought be given to the encouragement of acceptable behaviours as to the elimination of unacceptable behaviours. It is frequently the case that such behaviours are mutually exclusive. For example, it is not possible for a child to be out of his seat disrupting the work of another pupil if he is sitting at his desk engaged in a piece of writing. If he finds the production of disruptive behaviour more reward- ing than producing a piece of written work, then our task as teachers is to manipulate these contingent rewards so that satisfactory behaviour takes precedence over its opposite. The teaching of competing behaviours is a very effective strategy for change.

It is important to check that the competing behaviour that you would like to see the child produce is actually within his repertoire: that is to say, he can actually do it. There is obviously a great difference between the situation where a child does not perceive the need for a particular behaviour or, indeed, chooses not to produce it, and the situation where he cannot produce it even though he is trying as hard as he can. There are also differences for the programmes in these two situations. In the first, we are encouraging a child to produce the behaviour at the appropriate time. In the second, we are teaching both a new behaviour *and* when to use it — a more demanding task.

For example, a nursery teacher is concerned about a child not speak- ing at all in school, either to adults or to other children. If the child is talking normally to the other members of her family at home, both parents and siblings, then the programme designed to tackle this problem would be rather different to the one where the child is not talking at all, either at home or at school.

It should not be assumed that such skills deficits only refer to young children. Older children, adolescents and adults also may have some deficits. In recent years there has been a great deal of work carried out with adults in the field of social skills training designed to overcome such deficits. The following example illustrates the point well.

Clive, a tall, strapping 15-year-old, was frequently in trouble in his comprehensive school. He was variously described as 'insolent', 'cheeky' and 'too sure of himself'. These are rather vague descriptions of behaviour and need translating into behavioural terms. It so happened that whenever Clive was told off for a minor offence, he would look at the teacher silently, but smiling. This led to reactions on the part of the teachers and usually to Clive being in rather more trouble than might be expected from the original offence. This had the effect of creating a vicious circle as Clive then felt hard-done-by and often misbehaved subsequently. Fortunately, there was a social skills group within the school run by a teacher and a social worker. Clive's tutor discussed the problem with them and it was decided to try teaching Clive a new strategy. Clive and his tutor practis- ed a more appropriate way of behaving when being told off. He was not to smile but to keep a straight and slightly unhappy face. Additionally he was to look slightly downwards, establishing eye contact occasionally rather than staring at the teacher as he had done previously. This small change worked well for Clive who had not realised previously the effect of his behaviour. The result was that although he still got into minor trouble from time to time, teachers found him much easier to deal with and situations did not escalate as they had before, leaving Clive feeling rather more positive about his situation. He could accurately have been described as having a minor social skills deficit which had important consequences for him.

Skills deficits such as these may be much more common than many teachers realise. So the rule should be 'If in doubt, check if the skills are there.'

Increasing and Reducing Targets

It is necessary to consider the behaviour that is giving rise to concern from the point of view of whether it is desired to increase it in some way or to bring about a reduction. For instance, there may be concern expressed over an isolated child who makes virtually no contact with his peers. In this case the aim would be to bring about an increase in social interaction and we would refer to this as the *increase target*. The obverse of this would be to bring about a decrease in the number of occasions during the day when the child engages in solitary play or avoids group participation and this we would refer to as the *reduction target*.

Alternatively, the cause of concern might be that the child frequently wets in class. In this case the aim would be to reduce the number of occasions on which this occurs, and this we would refer to as the *reduction target*. The obverse of this would be to toilet appropriately. This we would refer to as the *increase target*.

The priority behaviour and the teaching target stated on the assessment chart should be written as such a pair of competing behaviours. You should select the behaviour that you wish to increase and insert this in the increase target box (No. 7) on the intervention chart (Figure 9.1). Similarly you should enter the behaviour that you wish to decrease in the reducation target box (No. 8 in Figure 9.1).

Make sure that for each target you have:

(a) chosen only one behaviour;
(b) specified the behaviour so that it is observable;

(c) stated your criteria for success, with intermediate targets, if thought to be necessary.

In our cumulative example the reduction target will be 'Will not start work when requested to do so' and the increase target will be 'Will start work on request with one reminder allowed'. Criterion: success on increase target 80 per cent of the time.

Study Activities

Write a series of 'steps to target' that you might use to bridge the gap between the priority behaviour and the teaching target for these two examples. Do not concern yourself with how you might encourage change but just set the targets that might be appropriate for the child.

(1) Jennifer is a four-year-old who started nursery school about a term ago. Her teacher and her mother are both concerned that she screams and cries for at least 20 minutes after her mother has left the nursery. Jennifer will not join in playing with any other children until she has quietened down. The teaching target that the teacher has set is: Jennifer will accept her mother's departure without fuss and join in with other children within 3 minutes of mother going.

(2) Anthony is a 12-year-old in his first term at the local comprehensive school. The problem is that he arrives at least 15 minutes late at the beginning of school every day. He never fails to arrive but can be up to an hour late on some occasions. The teaching target that his tutor has set is: Anthony will arrive on time to school every day, i.e. by 8.50 a.m. at the latest.

Guidelines for Study Activities

(1) Probably the simplest way of tackling this problem is to set a series of decreasing time targets for the screaming and crying, e.g. screams for 20 minutes → 15 minutes → 10 minutes → 5 minutes → no screams and joins in with the others.

(2) There are two main approaches possible for this problem:

(a) decrease how late Anthony is each day by setting targets, e.g. 15 minutes late → 10 → 5 → 0; or

(b) increase the number of days on time without worrying about how late he is on the other days, e.g. 0 days on time → 2 days → 4 → 5.

It may also be possible to combine these two methods and increase the number of days on time while also setting tighter limits on the other days.

10 CHANGING THE ANTECEDENTS

Figure 10.1: Intervention Chart. Changing the Antecedents

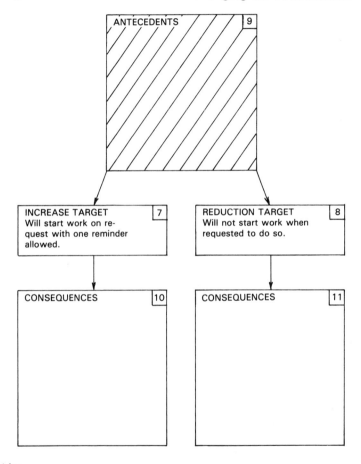

Aims

This chapter examines the antecedents of behaviour and the ways in which these may be manipulated in order to bring about desirable behavioural changes. After reading this chapter you will be able to complete the antecedents box (No. 9) of the intervention chart (Figure 10.1).

Changing the Antecedents

Assuming that the behavioural assessment in Part 2 has been success-fully carried out, there should already be information available in the assessment chart or on a separate ABC form regarding the antecedents that precede the behaviours that are giving rise to concern. Some note will also have been made as to the location and timing of these behaviours. It will come as no great surprise to note that with most children the pat-tern of behaviour may not be consistent throughout the week. Even the most 'disruptive' pupil in a comprehensive school has times when his behaviour is probably no worse than that of others in his class (however short these times may be). It may be noted also, again with secondary-aged pupils in particular, that some teachers have greater problems than do others with the same pupil. These observations serve to confirm our premise that events in the pupil's environment are important in helping determine his behaviour. The time of the week or subject content may affect it. The teacher's own behaviour will also affect it. This last obser-vation requires some clarification. We are not implying that a teacher may 'cause' disruptive behaviour in his class but that his behaviour will *affect* it.

Most behaviours, satisfactory or otherwise, are elicited by a cluster of circumstances or situational cues which may be usefully conceptualised as triggers. These behavioural triggers may be conveniently grouped in the following way:

(a) time variables;
(b) location and social setting;
(c) subject matter and task demands;
(d) teacher behaviour.

In order to decide how to alter the antecedents to effect behavioural change, it is necessary to examine carefully the data that have already been gathered. This should be done with a view to discovering whether there are any patterns to the behaviour that will provide a guide to deciding which antecedents to alter and how.

The following set of structured questions may prove helpful in discover-ing such patterns.

(a) Time Variables

Stated simply, 'Is the behaviour typically associated with a particular day of the week or times of the day?'

Day to Day.
On which days is the behaviour most frequent or intense?
Are these days consistent over a period of more than two weeks?
Are there no differences noted from the baseline?

Within the Day. Is the behaviour most noted at:
breaktimes/lunchtimes?
early morning?
after break?
after lunch?
at the end of the day?
no pattern noted?

(b) Location and Social Setting

General Location. Is the behaviour associated with:
closed classrooms?
open plan situations?
PE/games/gym?
craft/workshop areas?
outside?
other?
no pattern noted?

Within-class Location. Is the behaviour more noted when the pupil is:
near the teacher?
away from the teacher?
other?
no pattern noted?

Social Setting. If the pupil changes class during the week, is the behaviour associated with:
particular classes?
particular members of the class?
no pattern noted?

(c) Subject Matter and Task Demands

Subject Matter. Does the behaviour typically occur:
before certain subjects/activities?
during certain subjects/activities?
after certain subjects/activities?
no pattern noted?

Lesson Type. Is the behaviour associated with:
teacher-led work?
group work?
solo work?
discussions?
free time?
other?
no pattern noted?

Task Demands. Is the behaviour more noted when the pupil is working on tasks that he finds:
easy
difficult
other
no pattern noted?

Teacher Behaviour

If the pupil is taught by more than one teacher, as in a comprehensive school, then:
is the behaviour more noted with some teachers?
do these teachers have anything in common, e.g. age, sex, etc.?
no pattern noted?

General

Are there any other variables that appear to form a pattern?

The advantages of studying the patterns of antecedent events in such detail can be seen from the following brief example.

Jane was a second-year pupil in a city comprehensive. She was getting into an increasing amount of trouble for interrupting lessons and speaking sharply to teachers. Her teachers were very concerned about this as it was very much out of character. She had been almost a model pupil during her time at the school. A study was carried out of the times of the incidents and a very clear pattern emerged. The incidents, although they were in different lessons, were all in the periods before she had PE or games. Jane's tutor had a talk with her. It became apparent that she was very anxious about these subjects and in particular about having a shower and changing with the other girls. Discussions with Jane's PE teacher resulted in changes being made to her routine for changing. It was also arranged for Jane to talk to a teacher in personal studies about the 'facts of life', which finally resolved the problem.

Antecedents — Increase Target

While collecting the information regarding the antecedents of the problem behaviour, it is likely that it will have been noticed that a different
set of cues will trigger the acceptable behaviours. It is necessary to identify these cues in order that they can be taken into account when planning the intervention strategy. Careful observation will almost certainly
provide most of the answers.

Planning for Change

The objective when planning changes to the antecedents is that the increase target should be much more likely to occur than the decrease target.
The nature of the changes made will, of course, depend on the assessment and the nature of the problem. There is no easy 'cook-book'
approach that can guarantee success. However, the remainder of this section should serve to give an indication of the possibilities that could be
considered. Probably no programme would require all of them to be
manipulated but almost all programmes would need some of them to be
altered. The final choice must depend upon the nature of the problem,
the teacher and pupil concerned and the discussion that they have together
as part of the implementation of the programme.

Before tackling the antecedent events in the same order as listed at
the beginning of this chapter, there are two other important areas to discuss
first.

Personal Variables

We know that amount of sleep, diet and family interaction all may play
a powerful part in determining a pupil's performance. Therefore it needs
to be asked what possibilities exist for modifying the relevant factors.
The exercise in Part 1 concerning the extent of control and influence
should be borne in mind. Discussion with the pupil may lead to some
action. If, for example, a pupil is frequently in trouble over uncompleted
homework on one night of the week, then discussion may show that this
is the night that both parents are out and his older sister takes responsibility for the family. It might then be suggested that the pupil stays on
at school for half an hour or so to complete his work in the library before
returning to a less structured home environment under his sister's care.

One might go a step further with certain problems and actively involve the parents, e.g. with earlier bedtimes or in supervision with

homework. Actively linking the programme to home may help in many ways. It is a simple task to let the parents know of the pupil's progress, daily or weekly, via a record card. Letters home are another good tactic. All too often these only signify bad news and it comes as a very pleasant surprise to children and parents alike to receive a positive letter recording progress.

Even if you cannot alter the key events at home, as a result of your efforts a child may learn to respond more favourably to the condition over which you have some control within the school situation.

Rules and Instructions

The rules that are employed within a school system can be seen as a background to many problem behaviours. Rules exist at three levels within most schools. First, there are rules that the local Education Authority imposes, such as those relating to the use of PE equipment in the gym. Secondly, there are the rules that the school itself sets, usually by the senior staff. These tend to relate to general conduct around the school and standards of dress, etc. Lastly, and equally or more important, are the rules that individual teachers have about behaviour in their classes. The last set of rules will of course vary from teacher to teacher often quite widely, whereas the first two sets of rules *should* be enforced consistently by all members of staff. There are other codes that govern behaviour in schools. These are often referred to as routines. They are not rules as such but standard ways of doing things which ease the running of a class or a school and cause problems if they are not adhered to.

A few points should be borne in mind about the use of rules and routines.

(a) Rules should be few in number.
(b) Rules and routines should be made explicit to pupils.
(c) They should be worded positively in terms of what to do rather than what not to do.
(d) Both rules and routines should be followed consistently as a few occasions of not following them may slow their general learning quite dramatically.
(e) They should be easy to follow. If they are not, then they should be reconsidered.

Instructions should be clear and concise and specify for whom they are intended. The instruction 'Time for games. Girls first, go and get changed' is more likely to produce the intended result than the similar instruction 'Time for games. Go and get changed, girls first.' The last, crucial part of the instruction is likely to be lost in the noise of the boys stampeding for the door!

Similarly, if a child seems to have problems following instructions, then they can be personalised. For example, 'Right, class 3, John, are you ready? This is what we are going to do next.' Also, long complex instructions can be broken down into several smaller components resulting in enhanced comprehension by the pupil(s).

When changes are made to the antecedents, these will often involve changes to rules or to routines or to instructions or to any combination of these. It is essential that such changes be discussed with the pupil before they are implemented. He may well have some suggestions of his own to contribute that are useful. Additionally, such discussion may reduce or eliminate the period of 'testing out' the new rules or 'just seeing if you really mean it'. It is important to discuss with the child exactly what he is expected to do as, clearly, it would be quite unfair to expect the child to change his behaviour unless he knows what it is he is required to change and why.

It may be necessary to actually rehearse the behaviour as in a role play. If at all possible, the child should know what changes will occur to help him modify his behaviour. As part of the rules he should be made aware of what will happen if he displays the appropriate behaviour (increase target) and what will happen if he displays the inappropriate behaviour (decrease target). It helps if the child is aware of what he is trying to learn: this is an essential step in promoting cognitive behavioural change. This is obviously to be preferred to situations where a child is reacting almost blindly to things which are 'being done to him'.

There may be some circumstances when you might choose not to discuss the changes:

(a) if the child is very young, i.e. pre-school by age or mental development;
(b) if you are making only minor alterations to routine and you want to try them out first;
(c) if you think the pupil may react negatively to the suggestions, in a way which may not be in his best interests.

These circumstances would certainly constitute the minority of programmes and it should be stressed that, on balance, there is far more to gain from the active involvement of children in the management of their own difficulties than there is to be lost.

Prompts and Reminders

A very effective tactic is the use of a non-verbal signal to a child that acts as a prompt, reminder or warning about the rules, his behaviour or his progress. The advantage of a signal is that it builds in another stage before a rule or sanction needs to be applied and thus may prevent the escalation of a situation. The signal can be a private one between the child and the teacher such as: the teacher pointing at his watch — time is running out; a thumbs up — good so far; or a single finger raised — indicating that the behaviour has been noticed (and recorded).

It may also be a public signal similar to that used by football referees, a yellow card indicating a first warning and a red card meaning that further action will be taken — but not until the end of the lesson. Thus the flow of the lesson is not interrupted and very little verbal dialogue is needed.

Time Variables

Day-to-day. If you have noticed that a pupil performs better at certain times of the week than others, what action can you take? If the fluctuation is not associated with any other variable such as a particular lesson on a particular day, then you will need to discuss this with the pupil and/or his parents. If, for example, a pupil is generally worse on a Monday than on other days of the week, it may be the result of family tensions over the weekend. It may, in the case of a single parent family, be the result of a visit to the other parent. Alternatively, if the problems are on a Friday, then it may be anticipation of this visit. The possibilities are legion but some discussion may help.

A child may simply be tired and irritable by Friday, so what chances are there of rescheduling his workload within the week to take account of this?

Some situations will be easier to resolve than others. For those situations that cannot be resolved, the teacher's knowledge of them may lead to different handling or expectations, which allows the problem to be coped with rather than resolved.

Within Days. If it has been noticed that the pupil performs better at certain times of the day than at others, can alterations be made to his schedule or his tasks rearranged to take account of this? This is obviously easier to achieve within the primary-school situation. If, for instance, he appears to be an 'early morning' child whose performance deteriorates during the day, it probably makes sense to schedule the more demanding tasks for the time when he is at his best. This leaves the less demanding activities for the afternoon when his performance is more varied. Other children may be of the 'slow to warm up' variety and a different schedule may be appropriate for them. If doubt exists regarding which is the child's best time, it may be helpful to inquire of the child himself which time of the day he considers that he works best. Experience has shown that they are often well aware of this.

Location and Social Setting

General Location. If the problem behaviour is associated with particular settings, do possibilities exist for altering these, e.g. a closed classroom instead of an open-plan setting? If no such alterations can be affected, as in the case of PE lessons or breaktimes in the playground, is it possible to alter some of the other antecedents at this time, e.g. giving a short pep-talk as a reminder about the rules at the appropriate times or increasing the level or nature of the supervision?

Within-class Location. Does he perform better when seated near the teacher or further away from him? Are there any areas of the classroom which are particularly distracting, e.g. a window overlooking the games field?

Social Settings. If there are particular groupings of pupils which are unhelpful to him, can these be altered? For secondary schools where there are frequent changes of classrooms, it is perhaps worth considering having fixed places for the pupils in all the subject rooms. For some children it is worth considering some positive pairing, i.e. placing a less well behaved child next to a well behaved one who acts as a model for the appropriate behaviour. This is not always sufficient by itself, but in conjunction with positive reinforcement can be a successful ploy. You may need to observe if a pupil works better privately away from a group for some activities or better in a group or with a particular pupil.

Another variable to manipulate is the supervision within a setting. Does the pupil perform better if he is checked on frequently or if he is left undisturbed for longer periods of time?

Subject Matter and Task Demands

Subject Matter and Lesson Types. If the behaviour is associated with particular subjects or lesson formats, then it is necessary to ask what can be done to change these. The following range of questions may help:

Is the subject essential?
Can the lessons be organised differently?
Are there particular activities in the subject which cause problems?
Is the pupil interested in the subject?
Does he see it as relevant?
Should pupil participation be increased or decreased?

There are probably many more questions that could be asked and it is a useful exercise to give some consideration to these.

Task Demands. Most children gain satisfaction from the successful completion of a task but many are denied this because they are faced with demands that they cannot fulfil. It is important to arrange the difficulty and the quantity of the work set so that children are able to finish the task with success. Children may occasionally learn from their mistakes but they certainly learn more quickly and more happily from their successes. Don't we all! Decide, therefore on the following:

Should the amount of work be increased or decreased?
Should the level of difficulty be raised or lowered?
Should the level of accuracy expected be raised or lowered?
Does the child perform better in structured or unstructured activities?
Can the work be structured into smaller parts thus allowing more frequent feedback?
Does he perform better if the tasks are given definite time limits?

Teacher Behaviour

A teacher's total behaviour, both verbal and non-verbal, is absolutely critical in determining both individual and class behaviour. The skill of effective classroom behaviour management is one that takes time to acquire. Although some teachers rarely experience class or management problems even with the most difficult pupils, and are highly skilled, others experience more difficulties. It should not be thought that the first group of teachers have 'got it all worked out' and the other has not. Classroom management is a skill that can continually develop, as there is not yet a definition for a 'perfect teacher'.

Classroom management covers such areas as lesson preparation, formulation and application of classroom rules, use of clear instructions and reprimands, reinforcing good behaviour and performance, effective use of speech patterns and emphasis, and use of eye contact, body posture and territory. There are two key sayings to be borne in mind here: 'It's not just what you do but the way that you do it', and 'It's not just what you say, but the way that you say it.' The same action or saying carried out by two different teachers can have very different effects. This could be because of their status in the school (headteacher as opposed to classteacher), or their status in the eyes of the pupils based on their previous contact with them or the teacher's own confidence in the particular situation. This is a very complex and interesting area to which increasing attention is being paid. It is not possible within the scope of this book to do full justice to the subject. However, some guidelines and pointers are offered as a basis for teachers to examine their own practice critically but constructively. Teachers wishing to explore this topic in greater depth are directed to the recommended reading list at the end of the book.

A useful partition of this topic is into lesson preparation and organisation, and teacher behaviour in class.

Lesson Preparation and Organisation

Research findings have shown that in well organised lessons there are fewer behaviour problems displayed than in lessons that are badly organised. Some of the common factors are listed below. This should not be regarded as an exhaustive list. A number of the points may at first sight appear to apply mainly to secondary schools with subject-structured timetables but careful consideration will show that most points are, in fact, of direct relevance to the primary classroom as well. Teaching and management are more likely to be successful if:

At the beginning:

(a) Lessons are thoroughly prepared.
(b) The choice of work is appropriate to the age and ability of the pupils. This is especially important for lower ability pupils.
(c) Books, apparatus, etc., are ready for the beginning of the lesson.
(d) Homework and class work is regularly and carefully marked.
(e) The teacher is in the class first.
(f) The class knows the routine, ensuring an orderly and prompt start to the lesson.
(g) The work makes some intellectual demands on the pupils.
(h) Contingency plans have been made to provide activities for those

pupils who finish early and for those who may lose interest after completing only part of the lesson.

During the lesson:

(a) The objectives of the lesson are clearly stated.
(b) The lessons have an overall theme and teaching continuity.
(c) A variety of teaching methods, presentations and activities is used.
(d) There are no noticeable breaks in the lesson which could have been avoided.
(e) The pupils are sometimes expected to work in silence.
(f) The teacher uses questions as a means of keeping children alert and checking their understanding.
(g) The instructions used are clear and concise and employ language that is appropriate to the age and ability of the class.
(h) The teacher conveys her enthusiasm for the subject.
(i) Questions which require time for thinking or lengthy replies are saved until the class is well behaved and attentive.

At the end:

(a) Time is allowed to end the lesson in an orderly manner.
(b) Materials and equipment are put away in an organised way.
(c) The class are told how they have performed (feedback).
(d) Homework tasks are clearly explained.

Teacher Behaviour in Class

Communication within the classroom is a mixture of verbal and non-verbal behaviour. What we say is not the only part of the message. How we say it is equally important. Our use of posture, gesture, facial expressions and tone of voice are all very important in communicating our interest, moods, feelings, attitudes, etc. In short, they qualify what we are saying. The information they convey can be very important in the classroom situation. For example, they can inform a child that a teacher is angry or bored, nervous or confident, tense or happy, etc. Teachers need to be aware of these possibilities and to be able to control them as resources in their dealings with behaviour problems — both as a preventative measure and as a response in a situation.

In addition to communication within the class, teachers should be aware of their management of the space within the class in terms of seeing what is happening and being seen. The ability to appear as if you have 'eyes

in the back of your head' is a very powerful disincentive for misbehaviour!
When teaching, the children's attention can be better maintained by:

(a) standing prominently in the room;
(b) engaging in eye contact with individual children;
(c) using vocal variations reinforced by bodily movements and facial
    expressions;
(d) looking for and responding to feedback from the children.

Class behaviour is more easily maintained if:

(a) rules are few in number but made explicit to the children;
(b) they are applied consistently and above all firmly but fairly;
(c) they are worded in terms of what to do rather than what not to do;
(d) you are perceived as firm but fair.

Such measures reduce the opportunities for children to misbehave.
Reasoning and justification of your actions should take place at times
set aside for the purpose, rather than providing children with an alternative to work.

Challenges to your authority are more likely to be avoided by:

(a) standing prominently in the room;
(b) avoiding tension in body posture, facial expression and voice;
(c) using pupil's 'territory' in a confident manner;
(d) maintaining eye contact with pupils in a relaxed way (when not
    talking);
(e) controlling one's own responses by: not answering or giving eye
    contact to those who call out; choosing not to return smiles;
    resisting interruptions or dealing effectively with them;
(f) ensuring that the pupils respond to the teacher in some way;
(g) postponing disputes with pupils until they can be settled in private.

Such measures contribute to the impression that one's authority is
legitimate and are helpful when trying to create a controlled and attentive atmosphere in which to teach.

Teachers need at all times to be in control of their own reactions in
order to make full and effective use of the types of actions listed above.
In addition to these, many teachers will have developed other specific
ways of dealing with or preventing problems which have worked for them.
It is easy to overlook the wealth of experience that exists in most staff-

rooms. It can be difficult to ask for advice or to seek another opinion if one is experiencing difficulties with a child. If that can be done, then practical help is likely to ensue. As examples, the following strategies have all been offered by teachers as being 'tried, tested and approved' and also fit very comfortably with the other strategies outlined in this book.

(a) Give an early warning to a pupil. This can lessen the impact of bad news and allows the pupil a chance to amend his actions or to plan his remaining time more appropriately.

(b) Give good news with bad. This can avoid some of the side-effects associated with a reprimand. It becomes less like a punishment and more like feedback of results — something which can contain both good and bad news — and as such is likely to be easier to accept and more likely to be acted upon.

(c) Take care in situations that become confrontational to allow both sides a way out without loss of face. This means that both the teacher and the pupil should respect the other's position and not seek 'total victory' as this is likely to lead to resentment or a total refusal to give way. From such a situation there are then no winners.

(d) Extra care is needed when dealing with problems that occur in 'territory that belongs to the pupils', e.g. cloakrooms and toilets. If possible, move to neutral ground before discussing the problem in detail.

This is only a brief example of some of the practical suggestions that may be available from other colleagues. Further examples are given in some of the books recommended for further reading at the end of this book.

Study Activities

These study activities are designed to help you focus your attention on some of the methods that you are using now in managing your class(es).

(1) List up to five rules that you have for classroom behaviour. If they are worded in terms of what not to do, try to rewrite them in stating what to do.

(2) Imagine that it is the lesson immediately after morning break. The

children are coming into the class. What do you do to establish control at the beginning of this lesson? What methods do you use if they do not respond quickly?

(3) What techniques do you use during a lesson to maintain general class control that do not include direct verbal requests or instructions? List as many of these non-verbal cues, signals or gestures as you can. Examine the list. How many of these are positive and reinforcing to the pupils, i.e. indicating that you approve of what is happening? How many are negative, indicating your displeasure?

11 CHANGING THE CONSEQUENCES

Figure 11.1: Intervention Chart. Changing the Consequences

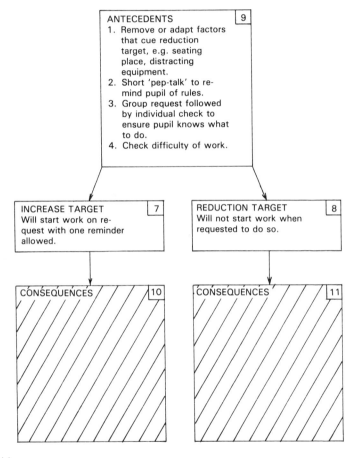

Aims

This chapter and the one that follows will together examine the ways in which consequences can be used to modify behaviour. After reading these chapters it will be possible to complete the consequences boxes (Nos 10 and 11) of the intervention chart (Figure 11.1).

Changing the Consequences

This section is the first of two that examine the various ways of altering consequences so as to influence behaviour. In this chapter we will be more concerned with the principles involved and some of the basic practicalities. The next chapter will look in more detail at some practical techniques that can be used in the classroom and in schools.

In Chapter 6 it was stated that those consequences that closely follow a behaviour can either strengthen or weaken that behaviour. Those consequences that strengthen behaviour and make it more likely to occur again in the future are known as *reinforcers*. Consequences that weaken behaviour, making it less likely to occur again, are called *punishers*.

Reinforcement is used to encourage and strengthen desired behaviours (increase target). Punishment is used to weaken or eliminate undesired behaviours (reduction target).

Punishment is not the only way in which behaviour can be weakened. Even without punishment, if reinforcement is withheld when previously it was given, the behaviour will weaken and tend to fall away. This is called *extinction*. A common example of this is the practice of ignoring a behaviour. Ignoring or not attending to inappropriate behaviours very often leads to the extinction of that behaviour. This is a very common technique used by many teachers and works best when it is the teacher's attention that is the reinforcement for the behaviour in the first place.

Reinforcement, punishment and extinction are the three main procedures in positive behaviour management which are used to modify pupil behaviour by controlling the consequences that follow behaviour.

There are two ways of reinforcing a child's behaviour:

(a) Giving something that is rewarding to the child for behaving in the appropriate manner, e.g. praise, privileges.
(b) Removing something that is unpleasant to the child for behaving in the appropriate manner, e.g. 'When you have finished your work, you may leave the desk in the corner.'

There are also two types of punishment:

(a) Giving the child something that is unpleasant for behaving in the inappropriate manner, e.g. shouting, ignoring, time out, detention.
(b) Taking away from the child a rewarding privilege for behaving in the inappropriate manner, e.g. not playing football, no playtime, etc.

The types of reinforcement and punishment are summarised in Figure 11.2.

Figure 11.2: Types of Reinforcement and Punishment

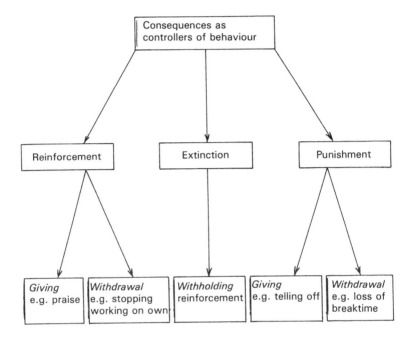

Although both antecedents and consequences affect behaviour, children usually *learn* a behaviour for the following reasons:

(a)   earning or maintaining a pleasant (reinforcing) situation or activity;
(b)   avoiding or ending an unpleasant (punishing) situation or activity.

Reinforcements

Reinforcers are contingent on appropriate behaviour (Grandma's Law), e.g. 'When you have eaten your pudding, you may go out to play.' A reinforcement is something that will increase the frequency or duration of a child's behaviour that was occurring when the reinforcement was given. Generally, if we are talking about reinforcement for appropriate behaviour, a reinforcement is something that a child will work for. This will vary from child to child. The reinforcement may be anything from 'Well done', a smile or a wink, to a privilege such as being first out to break to helping in the library.

This is more formally stated in the *Premack principle*, which states that any behaviour a child will readily engage in can be used to reinforce behaviour he will less readily engage in. The less-preferred activity needs to be performed before the more-preferred activity is allowed. For example, 'As soon as you finish your work you can go home'; 'When the whole class is sitting quietly, we can watch the television programme.'

Identifying Potential Reinforcers

Research has shown that reward systems are generally much more effective in encouraging good behaviour in the classroom than punishment, which often makes little difference. Pupil surveys have shown that, whereas school children agree with this finding, it has been much less widely accepted by teachers despite the accumulation of research evidence.

Rewards are likely to be most effective when:

(a) pupils can see they are related to good behaviour rather than randomly distributed by staff;
(b) they are dispensed immediately after positive behaviours occur rather than delayed;
(c) verbal praise of older children is given quietly: boys in particular tend to dislike public praise.

Non-verbal approval (smiles/eye contact/physical proximity) can be as effective as verbal praise. Although children seem to support the use of prizes as rewards, available evidence suggests this is more effective with academic achievement than behaviour. However, reinforcing academic performance can result in a decrease in incompatible disruptive behaviour in some pupils.

An action or reward is not reinforcing in its own right. It is only reinforcing if it is valued by the pupil and is perceived as rewarding by him. An action is only reinforcing if it encourages or strengthens the previous behaviour.

Deciding on appropriate positive reinforcers can be tricky since what may be a positive reinforcer for one pupil may be a negative reinforcer for another — *the trick is to know your pupil*. For example, lavish verbal praise may well be very reinforcing for a 6-year-old boy but the same action for a 16-year-old could have quite the opposite effect, especially if given in front of the rest of the class!

The systematic categorisation of reinforcers can take a number of different forms but one useful way of regarding them is as follows:

(a) Social reinforcement — non-verbal: hugs, smiles, winks, nods, 'thumbs-up', etc.

(b) Social reinforcement — verbal: all forms of praise or acknowledgement; 'That's great', 'Well done', 'Super piece of work', 'You've made a great effort', etc.

(c) Activities: being allowed to do something pleasant after a behaviour, e.g. playing football, extra playtime, computer games, etc.

(d) Privileges: being given a job or position that is valued by the child and that has some status, e.g. being a monitor.

(e) Tangible rewards: being given or using toys, games, books, presents from parents, etc.

(f) Consumables: food or drink, e.g. sweets, biscuits, 'pop', extra milk, etc.

(g) Token reinforcement: items which, although they are meaningless in their own right, have meaning within a given situation, e.g. ticks on a book or the figures 9/10 signing that the teacher is pleased; alternatively, actual tokens that can be exchanged at a later time for other types of reinforcers (see the next chapter for details).

There is no one right way to determine the appropriate reinforcers for a child. To a great extent this will depend on the teacher's knowledge of him, his likes and dislikes, the way he reacts to certain rewards and to praise, his age and interests, etc. Most teachers are well aware of the appropriate social reinforcers for a pupil but the other types may be less clear. There are three ways of finding reinforcers other than the normal social reinforcers:

(a) Observe the pupil to see what he chooses to do when he does not have to be doing something.

(b) Ask him what he would like to do if given a free choice.

(c) Ask his parents what his preferred activities are.

Children often announce their preferred activities when they suggest some classroom experience they want to indulge in. Preferred activities can function as reinforcers for less popular ones.

Rules for Giving Reinforcements

(1) Select a reinforcement that is the strongest possible, i.e. the one which is most pleasing to the child and will have the greatest effect on reproducing the appropriate behaviour. This will also mean that the reinforcement is appropriate to the individual child. However, the reinforcement must also be appropriate to the behaviour, e.g. a week off school may be a great reinforcer but it is hardly appropriate for good behaviour for one lesson!

(2) Reinforcements should be given as soon as possible after the appropriate behaviour has occurred. With younger children this means that the reward is given while the appropriate behaviour is occurring, not when it has stopped. It should be remembered that it is sometimes necessary to reinforce the absence of a particular behaviour. For example, with persistent behaviours such as rocking, head banging, inappropriate muttering, tantrum behaviours, etc., it is essential to be ready to apply the reinforcement as soon as there is a break in the behaviour. This piece of advice could be applied to good purpose by mothers whose babies continually cry!

(3) The delivery of reinforcements should be relatively generous at first and should then gradually diminish as the appropriate behaviour becomes firmly established.

(4) Reinforcements should be given with consistency and made explicit to the child if possible. For example, not 'Well done' but 'Well done, you remembered to close the door.'

(5) A reinforcement must *not* be given so frequently that the child becomes saturated and the effectiveness of the reinforcement becomes reduced.

(6) The reinforcement must not encourage behaviour that conflicts with the pattern of behaviour that you wish to establish with your programme. For example, don't reward a child for keeping to a diet with frequent bars of chocolate!

(7) The long-term aim should be to proceed from the use of consumable/tangible reinforcers to normal social reinforcement.

(8) The selection of reinforcements should be consistent with the age and sex of the pupil and with his own patterns of preferred activities.

(9) There should be a sufficiently large array of reinforces so that day-to-day fluctuations in interest can be allowed for, and so that no one reinforcer loses its appeal.

The reaction of many teachers on reading these rules might be 'Well, they're only common sense. I've been doing that for years.' We would agree they are common sense, but a few moments spent in self-examination are likely to reveal for most teachers that they only think that they have been carrying out all of them. Re-read them carefully, consider what is actually done in the classroom, and the majority of teachers will discover that there are one or two of these rules that are not part of their regular teaching style but with a little effort could be incorporated. The effort would be amply rewarded.

Punishment

Some Important Considerations

There are few topics in education as controversial as punishment. For many years educators have warned again and again that the use of punishment should be avoided. In fact, almost all parents and teachers make daily use of some kind of punishment, be it a well practised scowl, a sharp criticism or just ignoring the child.

Punishment is that which reduces the frequency of the behaviour which it follows. In order to decide whether a particular act is punitive, we must see whether the behaviour it follows undergoes a reduction in frequency. It is not *what* we do that tells us whether we are using punishment; it is only the effect that the act has on the learner that can indicate whether punishment is being used. Punishment depends on the effect on the child, as illustrated by the fact that a very withdrawn child might find lavish praise by his teacher a punishing event, i.e. the attention is a punishment.

The aim of using punishment is to eliminate or reduce undesirable behaviours. When behaviour is followed by an unsatisfying consequence, it is less likely to occur. The same effect can be produced by using rewards to increase behaviour incompatible with that which we want to eliminate, i.e. praise a child when he sits down; do *not* punish him when he stands up.

To recapitulate, there are two forms of punishment: presenting something unpleasant or taking away something pleasant.

Of the two forms of punishment, presenting something unpleasant is the least preferred form, but both forms have a number of important side-effects.

(a) Physical punishment seldom attaches only to the behaviour being punished. The person doing the punishing becomes steadily more disliked and aversive himself. He gradually loses his effectiveness as an agent for positive change.
(b) It produces strong emotional reactions that can interfere with learning.
(c) Punishment tells only what *not to do*, not *what to do*.

(d) It can serve as a model for aggression because children are more apt to do what they see the teacher *do* than to do what the teacher *says to do*.

(e) It may be a positive reinforcement through the rewarding aspects of the attention directed to the child.

(f) Excessive use of punishment is not really consistent with the goal that most teachers would agree with, i.e. learning should be an enjoyable and positive experience.

Rules for using punishment.

(a) It must be used in conjunction with a positive strategy designed to show and encourage the child what *to do*.

(b) Punishment should be used to interrupt the unwanted behaviour just long enough for it to be effective, e.g. time out for 2 minutes not 2 hours.

(c) Three things must be clearly understood by both teacher and child beforehand:
   (i) when it will occur;
   (ii) whether or not there will be a warning;
   (iii) what the punishment will be.

(d) It must be used *immediately, calmly* and *consistently*.

(e) Punish the behaviour, not the individual. Punishment should not be about punishing people, only their actions.

Inflicting pain (e.g. slapping), criticism (both verbal and non-verbal) and loss of privilege have all been used by teachers, some more frequently than others. The use of corporal punishment has, quite rightly, fallen into disrepute, not least of all because it is ineffective. The strategies of criticism and loss of privilege remain the two most frequently used by teachers to reduce unwanted behaviours. However, there is another way of achieving this result with some behaviours, particularly those which are dependent on teacher attention.

Extinction

Extinction is the procedure whereby behaviour which has previously been reinforced is no longer reinforced. If the behaviour does not disrupt the whole class and you feel that it is your attention which is maintaining the behaviour, you may be able to extinguish the behaviour by *ignoring it*. This is usually most effective with younger children for whom teacher attention is a very important factor.

For the procedure to be effective the following factors are important:

(a)   The behaviour must really be influenced by teacher attention. If not, ignoring it will have little effect and may even be interpreted as tacit approval.

(b)   Remember that the behaviour will not disappear rapidly. *In fact, it is often common for a temporary increase to occur in the rate and intensity of the behaviour at first while the child 'tests out' the new condition.*

(c)   Expect a spontaneous recovery of the behaviour a short while after it seems to have disappeared — but be extremely careful not to reinforce the behaviour.

Rules for Ignoring

(a)   No eye-to-eye contact.

(b)   Not saying 'Why are you not always good like that?'

(c)   Not saying 'I'm not paying any attention to that naughty boy.'

(d)   No request for child to go and do something else (diversionary).

Under the proper conditions, this method is extremely effective and has none of the side-effects of direct aversive punishment.

In many cases, especially at secondary level, the behaviour itself is disruptive to the whole class, and indeed part of the 'pay-off' of the behaviour is the attention of the class. In this case the behaviour cannot be safely ignored and other measures may need to be taken.

An Example of the Inappropriate use of Punishment

The following passage illustrates how an apparently punishing strategy adopted by a teacher in fact has the opposite effect, i.e. it is reinforcing. The passage 'The Criticism Trap', is taken from W.C. Becker's book, *Parents are Teachers*, published by Research Press in 1971.

The Criticism Trap

It was 9.30 a.m. The team-taught class had 48 children in it. Two rooms were available to the class, with a movable divider between them. The children's desks were grouped into 6 tables of 8 children each. They had been assigned work to do at their seats, while the 2 young teachers taught reading in small groups.

Two observers entered the room, sat down, and for the next 20 minutes they recorded the number of children out of their seats during each 10-second period. The observers also recorded how often the teachers told the children to sit down, or to get back to their seats.

During the first 6 days of observation about 3 children were out of their seats every 10 seconds.

The teachers would say 'Sit down' about 7 times in a 20-minute period.

The teachers were asked to tell the children to sit down more often. During the next 12 days the teachers said 'Sit down' 27.5 times each 20 minutes.

The children stood up more — on average 4.5 times in each 10 seconds.

The sequence was tried again for the next 8 days, the teachers went back to saying 'Sit down' only 7 times in 20 minutes. Out-of-seat behaviour declined to an average of 3 times every 10 seconds. Again the teachers were asked to tell the children to sit down more often (21.8 times in 20 minutes). Again the children stood up more — 4 times every 10 seconds.

Finally the teachers were asked to stop telling the children to sit down, but rather to praise sitting and working.

They did this and fewer than 2 children stood every 10 seconds, the lowest amount of standing observed.

The teachers saying 'Sit down' *followed* standing up. When the teacher said 'Sit down' more often, the children stood up more often. When the teacher said 'Sit down' less often the children stood up less often . . . saying 'Sit down' was a stimulus following a response which strengthens the response. It was a reinforcer for standing up.

To summarise, a child misbehaves, the teacher catches him and scolds him and he stops for the time being. Scolding seems to work. The teacher is rewarded for scolding and is therefore likely to do it again. The behaviour will increase so more scolding is needed: a vicious circle.

Practicalities of Rewards and Punishments

At this stage it is as well to summarise the use of rewards and punishments in the class and school. Reprimands or instructions which interrupt the children's activities are more likely to be successful if:

(a) they are given only when really necessary;
(b) eye contact is achieved before the message is given: children

should be silent and attentive;

(c) they are brief and as clear as possible;
(d) they are given as clear directives;
(e) bodily movements are limited when speaking;
(f) speech is delivered in 'measured' tone.

A teacher will be less likely to reinforce unwanted behaviour by:

(a) not following it with rewarding attention;
(b) discouraging peer-group attention;
(c) avoiding an emotional outburst;
(d) making it easier and more rewarding for pupils to do the work set than to avoid it.

Reprimands and punishments are more likely to suppress unwanted behaviour if they:

(a) interrupt the behaviour as early as possible;
(b) are consistently applied and enforced: threats should be backed up;
(c) are sufficiently disagreeable to discourage future misbehaviour;
(d) deal with the offence rather than the offenders; do not personalise reprimands.

Rewards are more likely to encourage desired behaviour if they:

(a) are given during the desired behaviour or as soon as possible thereafter;
(b) are applied consistently;
(c) are made explicit to the child.

The completion of a successful behaviour management programme relies on the careful selection of reinforcers and punishment to accompany the remainder of the changes planned, e.g. antecedents. There is no 'magic' way of determining these changes. It has to depend on the teacher's skill and his working knowledge of the child. No ready answers can be given, for no two problems are the same because no two children are identical. However, we all learn from our experiences, and knowledge gained from the past can help to facilitate finding the right programme for a pupil. The next section will examine some practical ways of using consequences in a programme and gives some advice on choosing a method.

Before we close this chapter, perhaps one question, which is almost always asked, should be answered. 'Won't using rewards in the class make

Table 11.1: Examples of Reinforcements and Punishments

Behaviour	Reinforcement	Punishment
Talking in class without permission.	Answering *or* making threats without carrying them out.	Not answering or punishing (e.g. by removing privileges or by time out).
Correctly answering question.	Saying immediately 'Good, that's right.'	Withholding approval/praise.
Failing to bring pencil, ruler, etc.	Allowing borrowing from other pupils or teacher.	Not allowing borrowing and/or instructing pupil to copy out work in own time.
Expressing disrespect to staff.	Entering into verbal discussion with pupil *or* giving lecture on bad manners.	Ignoring pupil *or* rapidly punishing without verbal interchange.
Repeatedly standing up/getting out of seat.	Telling pupil to sit down.	Ignoring pupil/praising when seated.

Remember: A reinforcer is any event which, when made contingent upon a behaviour, *increases* the chances of that behaviour occurring again. A punishment is any event which, when made contingent upon a behaviour, *decreases* the chances of that behaviour occurring again.

him different from the other children, and won't they all want them or resent that they are being given to a child who, quite often, has been a burden not only to the teacher but also to his peers?'

First, his behaviour is probably different or the teacher would not be thinking of using this approach with him! The other children almost certainly appreciate this already. Secondly, our experience and that of the teachers with whom we have worked has shown that children are much more flexible and accommodating than we ever give them credit for. They are capable of accepting different standards and handling strategies within both class and school for certain pupils. Indeed, in many instances they themselves become part of the programme, encouraging the pupil in question to meet his targets. This is especially true of primary-aged children. If any doubts exist about the other children's reaction to a programme, then be sure to explain it to them and, perhaps, attempt to involve them in it. The problems of using rewards in the classroom can be more in the minds of some teachers than in the behaviour of the pupils in the classroom.

Table 11.1 provides some examples of reinforcements commonly used by teachers.

Study Activities

(1) What are the three types of consequence that can be used to change behaviour?
(2) Using the categories on page 90, make a list of the reinforcers that you use with the children in your class. Are there any other reinforcers that are available within school but not within the class, e.g. praise from the headteacher for a good piece of work, or a letter of commendation?
(3) Make a list of the most common punishments that you use in the classroom on a day-to-day basis. It should include the minor actions such as a frown or a shake of the head. Then categorise them as being either giving something unpleasant or withdrawing something pleasant.

12 PRACTICAL APPROACHES

This chapter builds on the basic ideas of altering the consequences in order to change behaviour by developing a number of more specific techniques or uses of the general principles. This is very much a chapter that deals with working practice as all the techniques have been tried and tested. There are methods for encouraging or teaching behaviour, methods for reducing unwanted behaviour and methods that will do either.

Methods for Increasing Behaviour

As stated in the previous chapter, there are two main ways of increasing behaviour: giving something pleasant, e.g. praise, attention, toys, choice of activities, etc., or removing something unpleasant. Often, these strategies can be made more effective by coupling them with one or more of the following methods.

Discrimination Training

Should it be desired to teach a young child to react in a particular way in a given situation but not in another, inappropriate way, then it is necessary for him to learn how to distinguish between the two behaviours. For example, if it was desired to teach a nursery-aged child to take items from adults in a controlled manner rather than snatching them, it would be necessary to teach him to identify the differences between the two actions. When doing this, verbal and physical cues may be used. It is also very important that the preferred action is always reinforced whereas the unwanted action is never reinforced. In this way the child comes to identify the differences between the two actions and is most likely to perform the appropriate action.

Shaping

All too often the gap between the child's present behaviour and that desired is too large for him to bridge successfully or reliably, no matter how desirable the reward. The result is that he finds himself unable to reach the target reliably, becomes disillusioned or despondent and may even give up trying at all. The simple technique called shaping is one way of overcoming this. Shaping consists of successively reinforcing closer approximations to the target behaviour, i.e. using a series of steps to target. There are two ways of doing this, depending on the nature of the target behaviour.

(a) Progression in terms of frequency of behaviour, e.g. a child's targets for calling out in class may be reduced from thirty times a lesson to twenty to ten to five instead of from thirty straight to five.

(b) Progression in terms of exactness of the behaviour, e.g. if teaching a child to establish eye contact when talking to people, the successive targets could be starting from gazing at the floor to looking at the midriff to looking at the face to actually establishing eye contact.

Shaping has the great advantage of offering targets to the child that are always achievable throughout the programme. It is important to react to and reinforce each step to target in the same way that the target behaviour itself would be reinforced. This ensures frequent success and heightened motivation. It also makes it rather easier for the teacher to measure progress through the achievement of the 'steps to target'. It is a technique that can be applied easily within most programmes in one of the two ways noted, often to the benefit of all parties.

It is necessary, though, to plan carefully the size of the steps. Too large and the child will still fail. Too small and valuable time will be wasted by progressing through unnecessary steps. The keynote is flexibility. Be prepared to alter the size of the steps according to the progress of the child.

Care should also be taken only to reinforce progress in the right direction. Do not slip back to reinforcing an easier criterion than the current target. For example, if the pupil has reached a target of working for five minutes and the next target is eight minutes, do not slip back to giving the full reinforcement for only five minutes' work. You have clearly stated the rules: stick to them. This does not mean, of course, that you should not encourage the pupil at times less than five minutes by saying, for example, 'You're doing well'. However, if the reinforcement is five minutes' reading, then this is only earned by reaching the stated target.

Chaining

An allied technique to shaping is chaining, the name describing the technique accurately. It is useful when dealing with a complex behaviour that actually consists of several simpler component parts, e.g. tying up shoelaces or putting on a coat. The simple component behaviours are taught one at a time but are strung together to form a chain which, when compete, is the complex behaviour. For example, if the target behaviour were to teach a child to use a toilet, this complex task could be broken down into a number of simpler steps, e.g.

goes to toilet
pulls down clothes
uses toilet
uses tissue until clean
pulls up clothes
flushes toilet
washes hands
dries hands.

The individual steps within such a sequence can be taught and reinforced as if they were individual targets. The sequence can be tackled starting from either end. If the start is taught first, followed by working towards the final link in the chain, this is known as forward chaining. If the last link is the first taught, followed by working backwards through the sequence, this is known as backward chaining. This is often more successful than forward chaining because the child always finishes with the whole sequence completed even though he may not have carried out all of the steps himself. He can thus be reinforced as though for the completed task.

Chaining may be used in the teaching of social skills which often consist of a complex series of actions. An example of this might be the teaching of the skill of interrupting a conversation between two adults. This might be broken down as follows:

approach without speaking to the adults
stand close to but not within the personal space of the group
wait until one adult stops talking
say 'Excuse me' to one adult
turn to the adult you wish to talk to and say, 'I'm sorry to interrupt, etc.' (the actual words spoken are not crucial and would be appropriate for the child)

When using chaining it is important that the steps be described accurately to the pupil. The chain should also be forged using as many links as possible that are already within the pupil's repertoire. This reduces the teaching load.

Modelling

This is a very basic technique which most teachers use when teaching complex or intricate actions in their day-to-day teaching. For example, it is very common for a teacher to say in PE 'Watch John do a forward roll' and then point out the key parts of the performance. Exactly the same technique can be used to teach or modify behaviour. There is a lot of evidence to suggest that children learn complex skills or behaviours better through observation and reinforcement than through training by others. Children learn many skills and behaviours by observation of others, sometimes deliberately and sometimes quite by chance. By using this in a systematic manner, an effective technique for change becomes available.

It is important to choose an appropriate model for the task. In most instances the model should be of the same age and sex as the subject. He should also be of 'high status' as far as the subject is concerned, so that the subject would then wish to identify with the model and to behave in a similar fashion.

Modelling can be used either to teach new behaviour from scratch or to alter already existing patterns. It often needs to be combined with other techniques for complete success, e.g. shaping, chaining and rehearsal. Rehearsal of the behaviour may well be necessary for some children or for some skills. It is usually more appropriate for such rehearsals to be carried out in private first of all and then tried in the real-life situation. Frequent feedback about how well the child is doing is crucial to the rehearsal of modelling. Needless to say, frequent and appropriate reinforcement should be an integral part of this approach.

Charting Progress

All too often, verbal praise, social reinforcements such as smiles, and transitory non-tangible rewards may be of only temporary encouragement to a child. In such situations a permanent and tangible record of progress can be much more effective. This acts as a permanent reminder of past performance, progress and current goals.

Such recording should be initiated through negotiations with the child. If he can contribute ideas as to how it should be carried out, then more interest will be aroused and he will be immediately and actively involved in the system. How the recording is done is not as important as the active participation of the child and the visual representation of the progress. The child's role may be of a greater or lesser extent but should always be active. If the child both measures and records his own behaviour, then the technique is more properly known as self-monitoring progress. This is discussed in the next part of this chapter.

The following points should be noted when using this technique:

(a) The child should be involved in the devising of the charting system. This can be done through discussion with the child and by tapping his interests. The teacher should use both his own imagination and that of the child to raise his interest.

(b) Progress should be clearly shown in a visual form. This could be done on a bar chart, a graph, a game board or a picture which is gradually coloured in. It is important that teacher, child and possibly others can see the progress.

(c) The child should play some part in the charting process himself in a book or on a chart or merely by asking the teacher to record stars or ticks on a card.

(d) The system can grow and develop taking its cues from the child. Younger children in particular may need to start simply. The use of a charting system may for some children be a reward in its own right, but in some cases other rewards may need to be linked to satisfactory performance, e.g. 'When you have collected ten points, you can be first out to play for a week.'

As with all intervention strategies, the basic rules for giving rewards should be followed and in particular it should be made clear what the child has to do to earn the recording on the charts.

One very significant advantage of charting is that as the records are in a permanent state, they can be shared with others. For example, a child's record chart could be taken home on a daily basis in order that the parents are aware of progress and can play a part in the reinforcement process. This can be a very powerful part of an intervention strategy, as not only are parents usually the valued reinforcers as far as the child is concerned, but they also have access to more powerful rewards than do teachers in school, e.g. an extra half-hour of TV or going swimming at the weekend.

An Example of Charting Progress

Jamie, aged 3 years 6 months, attended the local nursery school. The staff were very concerned that after 6 months he still had not spoken to a member of staff. He had spoken on occasions to other children and it was reported by his mother that he spoke freely at home. His teacher took advantage of his interest in Dr Who, the television character, and drew a huge outline of a Tardis (Dr Who's spaceship) on paper and put this on the wall in the nursery. Jamie was told that if he answered a question put by her or asked her for something he would get a piece of the Tardis to stick on to the outline. The teacher made the responses easy for Jamie initially and gradually moved on to expecting him to initiate a question or conversation. A record was kept by dating each large piece as it was stuck on and of course the child could see his successes very clearly. The Tardis was completed within 2 weeks and, as a final reward, Jamie took the complete picture home.

Other methods of charting can be found in some of the case studies at the end of this book.

The methods so far discussed in this section have looked at ways of increasing behaviour. There will inevitably be occasions when simply reinforcing incompatible behaviour will not stop undesired behaviours occurring. In these instances we need to use punishment but in such a way that the negative aspects of it are reduced to a minimum. We have already discussed the drawbacks of giving something unpleasant as punishment, such as a telling off. The other form of punishment, that of loss of privilege, is to be preferred. It is often known as response cost, i.e. the child's inappropriate response costs him something he values.

Response Cost

This is a very commonly used sanction. Teachers and parents often withhold attention, approval and privileges in response to unwanted behaviour by a child. The aim is, of course, to reduce the likelihood of the child responding in the same way in future. There are several key points that need to be taken into account when using this method if it is to be used effectively.

(a) Some positive reinforcement must be available or there would not be anything to withdraw!

(b) The sanctions must be specified in advance. The child must know what he stands to gain or lose. Response cost must not come 'out of the blue'. To use it in such a way only devalues its effectiveness as an encourager of self-management.

(c) Avoid making the costs too high or the reinforcement too low. If this happens, the programme is likely to fail. The child will perceive that it is very difficult to gain anything and all too easy to lose everything. In extreme situations when a child has lost all his potential rewards, e.g. 'You're not going swimming for the rest of the term!', there is the great danger of provoking over-reaction and resentment. The teacher will temporarily lose her position as a positive-change agent and the child may well feel that he 'may as well be hung for a sheep as for a lamb'.

(d) If the cost is potentially one that is highly valued by the child, it makes sense to have stepping stones of warnings on the way to the loss of the privilege. Such incremental steps towards the loss instead of an 'all-or-nothing' approach increase the likelihood of the development of self-control on the part of the child.

(e) As with all behaviour management techniques, it is essential that response cost be applied consistently.

Response cost is often used in conjunction with other techniques, especially token economies, contracting and charting. Note that all of these methods have the benefit of specifying, in advance, the rules of the programme.

Time Out

There will be occasions when the rate of punishment or the response cost is likely to be so high that the teacher will feel 'I can't possibly punish him again.' Situations like this occur frequently and the usual result is either an especially heavy punishment or response cost to attempt to ensure that it will not happen again or, perhaps worse, ignoring the behaviour on that occasion. It is a very difficult decision for a teacher to make as none of us enjoys being negative with children. One important result of such a situation occurring is that all the consistency of the programme has vanished! One solution that can be employed with certain behaviours or situations is time out.

Time out is a ploy that will be instantly familiar to most teachers but here its use is described in a much more structured and systematic way than is usually the case. Time out is the removal of the child during or following the unwanted behaviour, to a non-reinforcing place for a brief period of time. This procedure can be used if the behaviour cannot be ignored as will be the case if the behaviour is adversely affecting others in the class or if there is some element of danger to the child or to other children, e.g. temper tantrums.

The success of the time-out procedure depends upon the following:

(a) The classroom must be a place where interesting things are happening, i.e. the child must find it a reinforcing (rewarding) place to be. Merely to send a child out from an unrewarding situation is simply to teach him to escape.

(b) The child *must* be sent to somewhere boring, i.e. an unrewarding place. Thus a busy corridor with plenty of activity and attention is *not* suitable. It may have to be under adult supervision and thus may be a part of the classroom where the child cannot see the activity going on in the room. It may be a small room or area of the classroom where an adult can keep an eye on the child without providing any attention or stimulation. The area of the room to which the child is sent must *not* be filled with interesting material and the child should *not* be allowed to take any books/pencils with him.

(c) Time out is *not* meant to be solitary confinement but an opportunity to interrupt the undesirable behaviour. The child should *not* be sent to time out for hours: five minutes is usually quite sufficient and ten minutes should be regarded as a maximum. Often even shorter periods have been found to be effective, e.g. two minutes.

(d) Removal of the child to time out should be effected as quickly and as *calmly* as possible with no further discussion.

(e) When the child returns from time out he begins with a *clean slate*. There should be no further mention of the preceding behaviour.

(f) Catch the child being good as soon as possible on his return from time out and reinforce by praise.

Figure 12.1 presents an example of the implementation of the time out procedure.

It is essential that time out be seen as part of a programme: it is not sufficient on its own. Reinforcement of acceptable behaviour in conjunction with time out is essential.

There are some practical difficulties with time out. In open-plan schools there is often no suitable room. It is also sometimes difficult to arrange supervision. These difficulties can be overcome by using an area

Figure 12.1: Implementation of Time Out Procedure

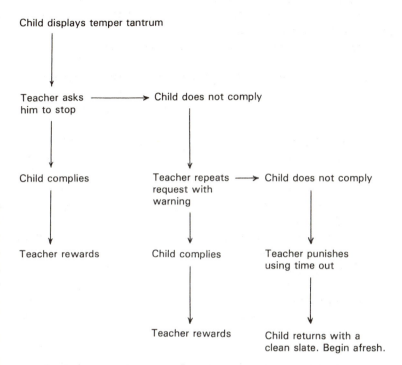

Child displays temper tantrum

Teacher asks him to stop ⟶ Child does not comply

Child complies

Teacher repeats request with warning ⟶ Child does not comply

Teacher rewards

Child complies

Teacher punishes using time out

Teacher rewards

Child returns with a clean slate. Begin afresh.

of the classroom screened off from the remainder. Occasionally a child may resist going, especially if he is in the middle of a temper tantrum. There are obvious physical limitations to the age or size of child with whom time out is applicable. However, it has been used with considerable success with nursery-, infant- and junior-aged children. With secondary-aged pupils it has been used in situations where the pupil himself is aware of the need for a cooling-off period. In these circumstances it is often used in conjunction with a self-monitoring programme, again looking at developing self-awareness and self-control. The time out period could be at the instigation of the teacher or the pupil or both.

Informal contracting, aimed at increasing self-control, can often be used within time out. For example, if a child is sent to time out during a temper tantrum and the normal period is six minutes, the verbal contract could be made, 'As soon as you are quiet for two minutes, you may return to the class.'

Contracting

A contract is a written agreement which states where, when and how a certain behaviour(s) will be carried out, what reinforcement will be given and possibly what sanctions may result if the contract is not adhered to. It is signed by all the people involved in the programme, i.e. teacher and pupil, or teacher, parent and pupil. For example:

(1) Roger will arrive at school on time (9 o'clock) each morning.
(2) Roger will come in from playtime with the other children in the class.
(3) If Roger does these two things, then Mrs Clarke will allow him to feed the school pets during choice time at the end of the afternoon.
(4) This contract starts on 12 May and will be reviewed on Friday 23 May.

Signed: Roger
                                                     Mrs Clarke

This is an example of a very simple, positively worded contract. It will be noticed that there are no sanctions built into the contract should Roger fail his targets. It is implicit that should he not arrive at school at 9.00 a.m., then he doesn't feed the pets that day. However, this is not stated and may lead to confusion or a difference of interpretation, something which should be avoided.

In order to avoid potential pitfalls, there are some simple rules that should be followed when using a contract.

(a) Contracts should be written in simple, easy-to-understand language. Contracts have for many years been used successfully with secondary-aged pupils but can be readily applied to older primary children if they are written in the appropriate language.
(b) The terms of the contract must be clear. It is important that they are written in such a way that they are readily understood by everyone concerned and that there is no room for misunderstanding or ambiguity. Remember that it is often more demanding to write a simple but watertight contract than it is to write a long,

complex and confusing one.

(c)   The terms should be fair, positive and negotiated. They should be fair in that both sides of the agreement should be, or should be perceived to be, of equal weight, i.e. no one side should be seen to be getting a 'good deal' at the expense of the other. They should be worded positively in line with the suggestions in the section on teaching targets. For example, it is better for Roger to 'arrive on time' for school than 'not to be late for school', as he is thereby encouraged to show positive behaviour. The terms should be negotiated because, as in other walks of life, contracts should be entered into freely with the terms being acceptable to all parties. This itself should prove to be a rewarding experience for everyone and very much in keeping with the concept of behaviour management rather than modification, for the pupil will play a part in determining his own contract. It should almost go without saying that all parties should agree the terms at the time of signing.

(d)   Good contracts in behaviour management, as in business, should contain bonus clauses for keeping to or surpassing the terms of the contract. They should also contain sanction clauses for failure to meet the responsibilities of the contract. However, this should only occur if all parties agree. They should operate for everyone — teachers and parents, not just children!

(e)   A contract should state a starting date and a finishing date. The finishing date may be the end of the contract or a time for reviewing it. It should be stated which.

(f)   Each person should read the contract and sign it to show agreement with its terms. Each person should have their own copy of the contract.

(g)   The contract must be honest. An honest contract is one which is carried out immediately and according to its terms.

A contract should be seen as part of a management programme, not as a programme in itself. Therefore the basic guidelines for behaviour management apply. For example:

(a)   Some of the rewards of a contract should be immediate or very soon after a behaviour has occurred. This is more important for younger children.

(b)   All reinforcement should come after the behaviour, i.e. 'When you have put away your toys you can watch the TV for an hour', not the other way round.

(c) Rewards should be frequent at first, diminishing in frequency as the behaviour is established.

(d) Contracts should follow for successively closer approximations to the desired behaviour. You may start by accepting a certain level of performance but tighten this up in successive contracts until the goal has been achieved.

(e) Rewards should be chosen in consultation with the child.

(f) The progress of the contract should be monitored and a date for review should be specified in the contract itself (see Roger's contract). For suggestions on monitoring progress, see Chapter 13.

Using Contracts

Contracts are a way of formalising a behaviour management programme; of involving the child in the design of the programme reminding all parties of their role in it. They are not programmes in themselves! You should therefore have completed all the stages in the assessment chart before deciding to use a contract. You will have selected targets and have recorded a baseline. It is then possible to plan the use of a contract in the intervention. The real difference that a contract brings to a management programme is that the information contained in the intervention chart is available to the child in the form of a contract and that the contract itself becomes one of the changed antecedents in the chart.

The stages in using a contract should be as follows:

(1) Complete the assessment chart.

(2) Negotiate standards for target behaviour and reinforcement with the child.

(3) Complete the intervention chart.

(4) Complete negotiation of the contract, specifying bonuses, sanctions and dates for starting, reviewing and finishing. Note that this may well involve people other than the teacher and the child: other teachers and parents who may have access to the most appropriate or more powerful rewards for the child.

(5) Draw up a contract which all parties sign and agree to implement.

(6) Monitor progress and trouble-shoot as necessary.

(7) At the end of the contract there are three possibilities:

(a) It is run as a 'one-off' and is terminated at the review date.
(b) It is amended in order to change the conditions because of the pupil's performance during the contract or to plug any loopholes and is then run again.
(c) With everyone's agreement it is run again in an unaltered form. At the end of the next run it may be discontinued, amended or continued.

As with any form of behaviour management technique, problems can occur. Some of the difficulties that may be experienced when using contracts are shared in common with other methods, e.g. the target behaviour was not clearly specified, the reinforcement was not valued by the child, or he simply tired of it. Details of these difficulties will be found in Chapter 11. However, there are some difficulties which are peculiar to contracting and these are now listed.

(a) Was the contract mutually negotiated?
(b) Were the terms of the contract clear?
(c) Did the pupil understand the contract?
(d) Was it fair, positive and honest?
(e) Was the bonus worthwhile?
(f) Were the sanctions too heavy?
(g) Did everyone have a copy?
(h) Is the child getting the reinforcement from another source?
(i) Have you or any parties to the contract kept to its terms honestly and consistently?
(j) Is your monitoring of the contract accurate, i.e. can you be sure about the pupil's behaviour or is the recording system not accurate?

The type of contracting discussed in this chapter is that of mutual negotiation. There is a further type, that of pupil-controlled contracting, in which the pupil determines his own task and reward.

Token Economies

A lot has been written about token economies and their use. It is important that the use of a token system be seen in perspective. A token economy consists of reinforcing a child's appropriate behaviour with tokens (counters, ticks, stars, squares coloured in on a chart, etc.), which can later be exchanged for other reinforcement. The tokens themselves may not have any intrinsic value but they are valued by the pupil because of what they represent and for what they can be exchanged. It is in essence a work/behaviour incentive system for children rather like the large-scale system that we all work in. We are paid tokens at the end of each week/month which in themselves are valueless — pieces of paper with pictures and numbers on them or even just numbers if we are paid by direct transactions to our bank. The paper itself is worthless. It is what we can do with the banknotes that matters.

There are certain advantages in using a token economy in some circumstances.

(a) They allow for behaviour to be reinforced at any time, i.e. they are simple and convenient to use, which may not be the case with the main reinforcer.

(b) If the reinforcer that a child is working for is large and infrequently given, e.g. a trip to the swimming baths, tokens can bridge the time gap between the behaviour and the reinforcement. The child knows that his behaviour has been noted and that the reward will be available at a later time.

(c) If there are difficulties in providing the reinforcement for a period of time, then the tokens can be used to fill the gap until it is available again.

(d) If a programme is being run for a number of pupils, then the use of tokens allow the same reinforcers at the time for all pupils but they can then be exchanged for different back-up reinforcers according to individual preferences. This makes it much simpler for the teacher to administer in the school situation.

Token economies are not applied in isolation. They must be part of an integrated programme, that is, linked to other reinforcers, or possibly punishment or response cost. Token economies are commonly linked with contracts and charting. An example of charting and tokens is shown in Figure 12.2.

Self-monitoring of Progress and Self-management

In certain situations it may be possible and indeed desirable for a child to monitor his own behaviour. This technique, known as self-monitoring, is a combination of the pupil measuring his own behaviour and charting

Figure 12.2: An Example of Charting and Tokens

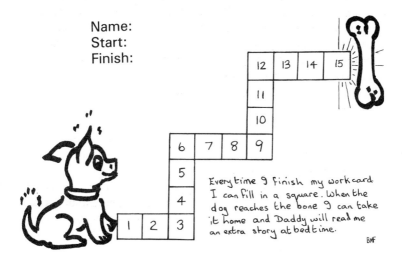

Name:
Start:
Finish:

| | | | |
|12|13|14|15|

11

10

| | | | |
|6|7|8|9|

5

4

| | | |
|1|2|3|

Every time I finish my work card
I can fill in a square. When the
dog reaches the bone I can take
it home and Daddy will read me
an extra story at bedtime.

BMF

it in some way. It is an especially useful technique with older pupils as it is a further step towards self-regulated and motivated change, a desirable goal for all of us, and away from change imposed by others, e.g. parents and teachers.

The two aspects of this technique, i.e. measuring behaviour and charting, are covered in other parts of this book, and thus only those aspects which are peculiar to self-monitoring will be discussed here.

It should be used only for behaviours that are easy to recognise and hard to overlook as far as the pupil is concerned. However, self-monitoring can have certain advantages over other forms of recording, in that it can be used for behaviours or feelings which are clearly apparent to the pupil but difficult or impossible for the teacher to spot, e.g. anger or feeling scared.

It should be an easy-to-understand and simple-to-complete recording system, which should appeal to the pupil. Its complexity, especially in terms of writing demands that are made, should take into account the pupil's ability and attainments. Thus diary formats, which are often used with success in this area, need to take into account the child's literacy skills.

Although the very act of self-monitoring his own behaviour can lead to change simply by focusing attention on it, the recording system should, at least initially, form part of an integrated programme, i.e. be linked to some reinforcement other than that obtained from the child recording his own success.

The setting up of a self-monitoring programme needs to be handled with some sensitivity if the targets are to remain clear. It is for this reason that a simple contract often forms part of the whole programme, acting as a reminder to all concerned about the target.

Prompts for the child to complete the monitoring system may be needed early on in the programme, especially with younger children, but this joint work is facilitated by the ease with which a self-monitoring system lends itself to close liaison between all the parties concerned. It is very important for a programme to be carefully monitored by an adult in the early stages to avoid difficulties arising. Therefore, an initial programme might run for a week rather than a month in the first instance. An example of a self-monitoring programme can be found in Chapter 15.

Self-monitoring of behaviour is very close to behavioural self-management. The aim of all behaviour management is to move from external control and reinforcement to internal control. A key step towards self-management is for the child to be able to assess his own behaviour accurately and to record it. This has been covered in charting and self-monitoring. The next step is to evaluate the behaviour. This usually involves the use of diaries. The aspects that should be covered are as follows.

(a) The pupil keeps a diary or log of events. This should be restricted to events that are perceived as relevant to the presenting difficulty.
(b) He notes down what happened, what was said and what he did.
(c) He also notes what the circumstances were that led up to the event.
(d) The pupil then records how he felt before, during and after the event. Did he feel comfortable or uncomfortable, happy or sad, calm or angry, etc.? It is sometimes helpful to suggest polar constructs such as these to make the evaluation easier.
(e) Was he satisfied or not with the way in which he reacted in the situation?
(f) Plan changes. What can be done to avoid or create such situations in the future? What could he have done differently in the actual situation?

Often the pupil will need to discuss the findings with someone else in a positive and supportive way. The quality of the diary kept will help determine how easy and productive that help is. Some diary formats that have been used for different circumstances are given in Chapter 15 to act as a guide. They should not be copied slavishly. Rather, use them as a basis for designing a format that is appropriate to the circumstances of self-monitoring and self-management with or without teacher support for the recording.

Selecting a Method for Change

It will not have escaped the reader's notice that the majority of techniques and approaches discussed in this chapter have been geared to the increase of desirable behaviours. Apart from being preferred from an ethnical point of view, this should also be seen in relation to the strategy of the incompatibility of the increase and reduction targets. Increasing one will automatically reduce the other.

Before dealing with the finer points of choosing a method, a few general points must be made.

(a) The method chosen must be practical. It should be easy for the teacher to remember to give the reinforcement. The rules should be simple to explain and to adhere to. If a token economy is to be used, do not make it any more complicated than it needs to be in order for it to work.

(b) The method chosen should be realistic. Do not link in major reinforcers that may not be available, e.g. school trips, etc. Their failure to materialise will ruin the consistency of the programme.

(c) The method should be generally compatible with the classroom organisation and the teacher's practice. This does not mean that nothing new or different should be attempted. Rather, choose a method that is comfortable and that is likely to be used with consistency.

(d) Whatever is chosen, it must be used consistently. This is vitally important. Research has shown that the rate of learning/behavioural change is much higher if the handling is consistently applied.

(e) The level of intervention needs to be carefully matched to the severity of the problem. Again, we would not want to see sledgehammers used for cracking walnuts. For instance, a class-based token economy system backed up by a contract would be excessive in trying to stop one child chewing his pencil! Quite low levels of behavioural intervention can be very effective when used in a structured and consistent manner. One piece of research reports that a 'light' intervention consisting of rules, praise, ignoring and free time for work achieved raised the average 'on-task' behaviour from 55 per cent to between 90 and 95 per cent. This was not with a co-operative class of 9-year-olds, but with a difficult class of 14- to 15-year-olds who were selected because of the difficulties that they created for teachers in that school.

(f) If a 'heavy' method of intervention is used first and it is not successful, then the teacher is left with fewer options for future interventions. By choosing a method that is gauged to be just strong enough to work, maximum flexibility of options is maintained.

Planning for Change

Just as in the case of planning for antecedent change (Chapter 10), it is necessary to look closely at what actually happens before deciding what to do instead.

In the case of planning for change of the consequences, there are two sets of actions to consider: what happens after the increase behaviour, and what happens after the reduction behaviour.

Reduction Target. In this case most of the data you need should already be noted on the assessment chart. In particular:

What do you normally do when the child produces the reduction target behaviour?

What do the other pupils do in response to the reduction target behaviour?

What effect does the reduction target have on the completion of work or its quality?

What does the child do after the behaviour?

Increase Target. In most, if not all, instances there are social consequences that follow from the production of unsatisfactory behaviour. Much less consistent and certain are the consequences that follow desired behaviour. Children may work successfully, attentively, quietly and co-operatively, and the most likely consequences of all this desirable behaviour is that it will be ignored. The question should, therefore, be asked:

What does the teacher do when increase target behaviour occurs?
What do the other children do when increase target behaviour occurs?
What does the child do after the increase target behaviour?

The Changes

Reduction target consequences. Decide precisely what will follow the reduction target behaviour should it occur. This could take many forms, for example: withdrawal of reward; behaviour ignored; application of punishment; time out. Other examples of these are given on pages 98 and 104–8.

Whatever strategy is adopted — and it may be a combination of the suggestions given here — it is absolutely crucial that it should be applied consistently. It is on this point that the success or failure of the strategy will rest. The exact choice of what form each may take is entirely child-specific. What is punishing for one child may not be for another.

Increase Target Consequences. Decide which consequences can be modified or introduced to provide the appropriate reinforcement for the increase target.

(a) What reinforcements will be given for what behaviour?
(b) How is the reinforcement going to be given?
(c) What schedule of reinforcement is going to be used, i.e. how frequently?
(d) How is social reinforcement and praise to be given?

Item (d) is all-important. All reinforcements must be accompanied by social reinforcements, e.g. verbal praise, as the aim is to work towards this type of reinforcement becoming the most powerful. Eventually, self-administered social reinforcement is achieved for some people, i.e. job satisfaction, pleasure in social interaction, pleasure at giving pleasure to others, etc.

Summary

Behaviour management is a very subtle skill. It is not always possible to get it right first time. Indeed experienced users of the techniques are aware that the aim is to get the programme approximately correct in the first instance, implement it and then 'fine tune' it as it is running. This 'getting it right by seeing how it's going' is an essential part of any programme and is the subject of the next chapter.

The close monitoring of the child's reactions and progress is important because what a teacher thought would be rewarding may turn out not to be so. It is not possible to give any hard and fast guidelines for what methods to use with which children or which problems. They are all different and so are the teachers implementing the programmes and their relationships with the children. However, experience has shown that generally teachers have developed a good sense of what is appropriate from their close working experience with children. Such practical experience is very valuable and can be enhanced and made more effective by using the kind of structured approaches outlined in this book. Above all a teacher should not become despondent if a programme does not work first time — try again! It only goes to show what complicated creatures human beings are — even the little ones. Anyway, wouldn't life by boring if it were all predictable?

13 MONITORING PROGRESS AND MAINTAINING BEHAVIOUR

Figure 13.1: Intervention Chart. Monitoring Progress and Maintaining Behaviour

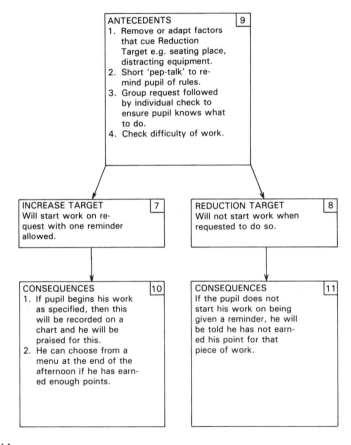

ANTECEDENTS [9]
1. Remove or adapt factors that cue Reduction Target e.g. seating place, distracting equipment.
2. Short 'pep-talk' to remind pupil of rules.
3. Group request followed by individual check to ensure pupil knows what to do.
4. Check difficulty of work.

INCREASE TARGET [7]
Will start work on request with one reminder allowed.

REDUCTION TARGET [8]
Will not start work when requested to do so.

CONSEQUENCES [10]
1. If pupil begins his work as specified, then this will be recorded on a chart and he will be praised for this.
2. He can choose from a menu at the end of the afternoon if he has earned enough points.

CONSEQUENCES [11]
If the pupil does not start his work on being given a reminder, he will be told he has not earned his point for that piece of work.

Aims

This chapter deals with the evaluation of an intervention programme once it has begun. After reading this section you will be able to choose an appropriate method of evaluation.

Monitoring Progress

We have now reached the stage of having completed our assessment chart and have decided on the strategies for change to be used as shown in the intervention chart (Figure 13.1).

It is not enough just to decide on an intervention programme: its success must be evaluated. Just as careful observation and measurement are important in establishing a baseline for problem behaviour, continuation of these monitoring procedures is important in determining the success or otherwise of any intervention strategy introduced in order to effect some kind of behaviour change.

To check whether the programme is having the intended effects, the teacher should evaluate the usefulness of the behaviour techniques used in the intervention phase of the programme. This is important for three reasons:

(a) To clarify how the teacher's behaviour is affecting the pupil. Obviously, you need to know whether your strategies are being successful; if not, you should change them. You should not be discouraged; it is quite likely that there will be practical problems. For example, what you at first think may be rewarding may turn out not to be so.

(b) To alert the teacher to gradual changes in pupil behaviour which might not otherwise be apparent. Dramatic changes don't always happen. You may find yourself saying 'He's still doing it!' However, careful management may show that he no longer calls out 20 times in a lesson but only five times. He *is* still doing it, but there is evidence of significant progress towards the ultimate goal. Teachers need to know how well they are doing in order to maintain their own motivation to continue.

(c) To provide feedback to the pupil. Just as in point (b), a knowledge of results and success plays an important part in maintaining his motivation for change.

There are two ways of evaluating a programme — periodically and continually.

Periodic Evaluation

This simply consists of remeasuring the behaviour using the same methods that were used when completing the assessment chart. For instance, you might decide to remeasure after one week, three weeks and five weeks.

If you charted the results, you might get a graph such as is shown in Figure 13.2.

Figure 13.2: Periodic Evaluation Graph

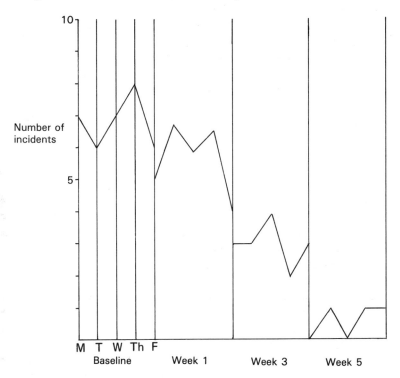

Obviously there has been a significant improvement over the five-week period. It is up to you, with your knowledge of the programme and the child, to decide how frequently to remeasure the behaviour. You must also decide whether to measure the reduction target or the increase target. If you are intending to discuss the results with the child, it is more positive if you measure the increase target, as you are encouraging him 'What to do' rather than 'What not to do'.

Continual Evaluation

Continual evaluation might sound as though it is extremely time consuming, but in fact quite the opposite is true. It is often possible to set up a recording system in which the child plays a significant part. The recording system can act as a permanent record of what is happening day to day. In many cases the recording system can act as part of the reward system. For example, the chart shown in Figure 13.3 was used to record the number of completed pieces of work that a child produced. The rewards for completing each piece of work were verbal praise and a star to go on to the chart. As the weekly chart is divided up into days, progress can be seen day to day and, by comparing charts week to week, the progress is seen by both child and teacher.

Figure 13.3: Continual Evaluation Chart

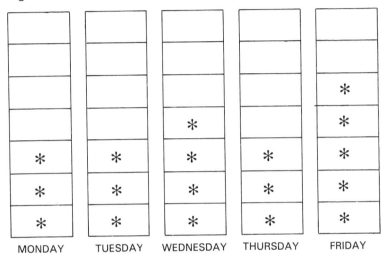

Again it is more positive as far as the child is concerned to record the increase target. In this way he can be encouraged to beat 'yesterday's score' or 'last week's total'.

Maintaining the Behaviour

Up to this point in the book we have assessed behaviour, decided upon a target behaviour and designed our intervention strategies. In most instances the target behaviour will have been selected from among three or four measured behaviours and attention will have been focused almost entirely upon this.

The aim of the intervention strategy is to eventually place the responsibility for the control of the target behaviour on to the child, and in order to achieve this it is necessary to arrange for the programme to be phased out. This can be achieved by a combination of methods. For instance, in our cumulative example the child received a point when he achieved the target behaviour, i.e. commencing work on request with one reminder allowed. At the start of the programme it could have been decided that six points must be attained to allow him to choose an activity from among a menu of preferred activities. As the programme proceeded successfully, the number of points required could have been increased to nine or ten. Alternatively, the target behaviour could have been changed so that no reminders were allowed or only an average of one reminder out of two occasions.

If the programme is not successful, then it would be necessary to reduce the number of points required to earn the preferred activity before going on to phase out the programme.

Remember, we are only interested in success and it is our responsibility to change the consequences as necessary in order to achieve this.

Remember also that praise, encouragement and positive attention, i.e. social reinforcement, must always accompany the more concrete rewards as the aim is for the former to replace the latter.

As the intervention strategy proceeds, there will come a time when you are satisfied with the change that has been brought about in the target behaviour. This is likely to be when it attains a point where it is commensurate with the accepted standard for the group.

It may now be necessary to focus attention upon the next most troublesome behaviour and to examine this in the same analytical way that was used for the first behaviour. However, much of the preparatory work will already have been carried out when the original assessment was made. It may be necessary to decide upon the intervention strategy.

What is most likely, however, is that the positive approach that was adopted towards the first behaviour will have had an affect upon the total behaviour of the child.

A second intervention is also likely to be easier than the first for three reasons:

(a) The child will have experienced success and become aware that his behaviour can change.
(b) You will already be aware of which tactics are most successful.
(c) You will have experienced success in changing behaviours.

In conclusion, these are three important points to remember:

(a) Always link social reinforcement to tangible rewards.
(b) Gradually fade out the tangible rewards but ensure that the child remains successful. Retain the social reinforcement.
(c) Use the experience gained to design subsequent programmes.

PART 4:

POSITIVE BEHAVIOUR MANAGEMENT IN PRACTICE

14 STEP-BY-STEP GUIDE TO POSITIVE BEHAVIOUR MANAGEMENT

This section provides a step-by-step guide to behaviour management which you can use as a checklist for completion of your programme. It also provides a reminder of some of the key points in behaviour management.

Assessment

Step 1

(1) In selecting the problem behaviour have you:

	Yes	No
(a) Selected behaviours that are observable and measurable?		
(b) Entered these behaviours in the behaviour box (No. 1)?		

(2) In measuring the behaviour have you:

(a) Decided for each behaviour whether it is a problem of frequency or duration?		
(b) Selected a specific method for measuring?		
(c) Chosen the time(s) of day to measure the behaviour?		
(d) Entered the results in the measurement box (No. 2)?		

Step 2

(1) In selecting the priority behaviour have you:

(a) Selected a behaviour where the intervention is likely to be successful?		
(b) Selected a behaviour which may influence other behaviours?		
(c) Entered the chosen behaviour in the priority behaviour box (No. 3)?		

Step 3

(1) In noting the antecedents have you:

    (a) Recorded the subject matter?

    (b) Recorded the social and teaching environment?

    (c) Recorded any other significant circumstances?

    (d) Entered this information in the antecedents box (No. 4)?

(2) In noting the consequences have you:

    (a) Recorded your own response(s)?

    (b) Recorded the other children's reactions?

    (c) Indicated the child's subsequent behaviours?

    (d) Entered this information in the consequences box (No. 5)? ·

Step 4

(1) In selecting the teaching target have you:

    (a) Chosen a target that is incompatible with the priority behaviour?

    (b) Worded it positively?

    (c) Entered it into the teaching target box (No. 6)?

(2) In deciding on the targets for the intervention have you:

    (a) Completed the reduction target box (No. 7)?

    (b) Completed the increase target box (No. 8)?

Intervention

Step 5

(1) In designing the antecedents section of the intervention have you:

    (a) Specified any work/activity changes?

    (b) Changed the social/physical/teaching environment?

    (c) Modified your own strategies/behaviour?

    (d) Entered this information in the antecedents box (No. 9)?

Yes	No

(2) In designing the decrease target consequences have you:

    Yes   No

  (a) Decided what consequences will follow the decrease target behaviour?

  (b) Decided whether a warning/signal will be given?

  (c) Entered this information in the consequences box (No. 11)?

(3) In designing the increase target consequences have you:

  (a) Decided how to reinforce the increase target?

  (b) Decided on a reinforcement schedule?

  (c) Decided how to link this with social reinforcement?

  (d) Planned how and when to give the reinforcement?

  (e) Entered this information in the consequences box (No. 10)?

(4) In planning the intervention have you:

  (a) Fully involved the child in the planning and discussion?

  (b) Discussed the intervention with the child's parents or involved them in it?

Step 6

(1) Have you decided on a method for monitoring the progress of the intervention?

15 CASE STUDIES

This chapter consists of some case studies and the programmes that have been used by teachers in dealing with the problem behaviours. The first two case studies are presented in rather fuller detail than the remainder and include sample assessment and intervention charts.

Raymond M____

Raymond is an adopted child who was ten years old when it was first decided to attempt to bring about some change in his uncontrolled and sometimes bizarre behaviour. Raymond has attended the same school since commencing nursery and he has been in the care of a succession of teachers all of whom have experienced similar difficulties in controlling his behaviour. All these teachers have been unanimous in describing Raymond as a very pleasant boy, and the general consensus of opinion seemed to ascribe his difficult behaviour to factors largely outside his own control. His adoptive parents were always described in the warmest terms by the staff of the school and it seemed that they were always ready to co-operate with any suggestions put forward by them. Raymond's behaviour at home also gave rise to concern for his parents. Mr and Mrs ____ knew few details of Raymond's background before he came to them for adoption but they suspected that it had been fraught with difficulties and they tended to ascribe his uncontrolled and inconsequential behaviour to his early experiences.

A few weeks prior to the decision being made to make a systematic effort to help Raymond to achieve more control over his actions, the whole school staff had attended a one-day course on positive behaviour management mounted by the local schools psychological service. It was hoped that teachers would be prepared to try out some of the ideas and methods that had been discussed, and in order to encourage them to do so an undertaking was given by the psychologists to come quickly to their aid if they found themselves to be in difficulties or if they found that the programme they had devised was proving to be unsuccessful.

This was precisely what occurred in the case of Raymond. His teacher, a very warm and sensitive young woman of considerable enthusiasm and skill, had set up a programme which had produced a transitory improvement in Raymond's behaviour but which had to be abandoned because it had ceased to interest him or to motivate him towards change. When the details of the programme were discussed with the teacher it soon became apparent that there were a number of factors operating which had led to its failure. First, no accurate observations had been made of Raymond's behaviour so that it was not possible to state with any certainty which out of a list of five or six was the priority behaviour. Secondly, the target behaviour chosen was the one most difficult to control without drawing the attention of the rest of the class to it. Thirdly, the target that had to be achieved in order to obtain the reward was virtually unattainable for Raymond as he was required to produce the target behaviour for a whole day with no failures allowed. It was also suspected that the reward on offer was not regarded as being sufficiently valuable to be worth all the effort. Subsequently, this was found not to be so as Raymond valued very highly the 'Well done' badge given out by the headmaster.

It was decided to go right back to the beginning again and this time to make all the necessary observations on the behaviours identified and to complete the assessment chart fully before going on to the intervention chart. It was also decided to brief Raymond's parents fully with regard to what was being done, and to involve them in the reinforcement plan when the programme was started.

Although the teacher knew Raymond very well, it was thought to be important for her to watch him closely for a day after which she would make a list of the behaviours she had *actually observed* which gave her cause for concern. During the day of observation a list of five behaviours was produced, as follows:

(a) Calling out. This was not just calling out answers or questions but often involved the production of a running commentary (often amusing) on what was being said by the teacher.
(b) Inappropriate movement. This ranged from adopting contorted positions on the chair while working to actually crawling under desks and chairs while a lesson was in progress.
(c) Leaving place. This varied from leaving his place to ask the teacher a question to walking across to other children and interfering with their work.
(d) Making noises. Most of these were incomprehensible and ranged in volume from shouts to whispers.
(e) Repetition of instructions. Rarely did Raymond commence a piece of work without seeking one or more repetitions of the instructions given to the class.

Figure 15.1: Observation Chart, Raymond M____

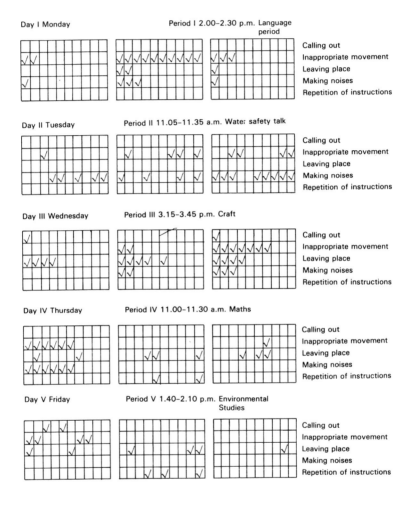

These five behaviours were entered on an observation chart. A profile of Raymond's behaviour in these areas was obtained for a period of one week, for half an hour each day, in five different activities at five different times of day. When a behaviour occurred in a particular one-minute period, a tick was put in the appropriate box. It was possible to have an independent observer in the classroom for each of these periods. The results of these observations can be seen in Figure 15.1. Rates per hour were calculated for the five behaviours as follows.

	Total	Time (hours)	Rate
Calling out	4	2.5	1.6
Inappropriate movement	44	2.5	17.6
Leaving place	30	2.5	12
Making noises	33	2.5	13.2
Repetition of instructions	5	2.5	2

Some considerable thought was given as to which of these five behaviours should be selected as the priority behaviour and for a number of reasons it was decided to take 'leaving place'. If success were achieved in decreasing the rate of this behaviour, it must automatically have a decreasing effect on some of the 'inappropriate movements'. It was an easy behaviour for the teacher to observe and to count. It was an easier behaviour for Raymond to be aware of himself than, for example 'making noises'.

The 'antecedents' and the 'consequences' cells of the assessment chart were then filled in as shown in Figure 15.2 and the 'teaching target' was discussed and formulated. This target was seen to be extremely important because it was on the faulty selection of this that the previous programme had foundered. It was vital to bear in mind that the whole aim of the positive behaviour management approach is for both the child and the teacher to experience success and for that success to be maintained. It was, therefore, essential to set the teaching target at a level that the child would achieve. At the time when the baseline was taken, the rate for this behaviour was running at 12 times each hour so it seemed reasonable to start off with a target of half this rate but sustained for only half an hour, i.e. 'to remain in place for half an hour — three failures allowed'. This represented the main target but there was a subsidiary target that entailed achieving the daily target on three days out of five.

The intervention chart was then filled in as shown in Figure 15.3. It can be seen that part of the 'antecedents' included the method of

Figure 15.2: Assessment Chart, Raymond M____

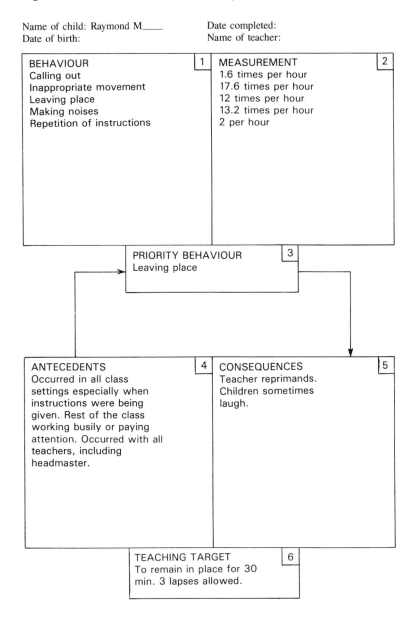

Name of child: Raymond M____   Date completed:
Date of birth: Name of teacher:

BEHAVIOUR	1	MEASUREMENT	2
Calling out		1.6 times per hour	
Inappropriate movement		17.6 times per hour	
Leaving place		12 times per hour	
Making noises		13.2 times per hour	
Repetition of instructions		2 per hour	

PRIORITY BEHAVIOUR 3
Leaving place

ANTECEDENTS	4	CONSEQUENCES	5
Occurred in all class settings especially when instructions were being given. Rest of the class working busily or paying attention. Occurred with all teachers, including headmaster.		Teacher reprimands. Children sometimes laugh.	

TEACHING TARGET 6
To remain in place for 30 min. 3 lapses allowed.

Figure 15.3: Intervention Chart, Raymond M____

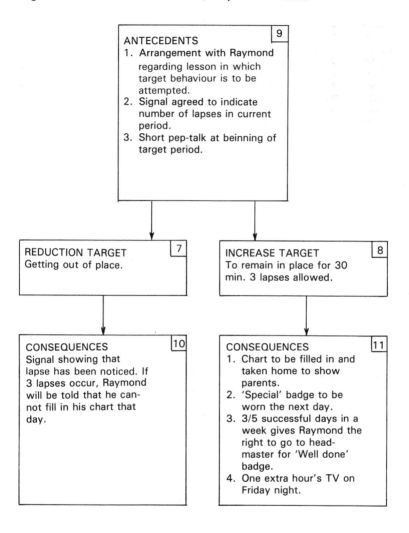

ANTECEDENTS   9
1. Arrangement with Raymond regarding lesson in which target behaviour is to be attempted.
2. Signal agreed to indicate number of lapses in current period.
3. Short pep-talk at beinning of target period.

REDUCTION TARGET   7
Getting out of place.

INCREASE TARGET   8
To remain in place for 30 min. 3 lapses allowed.

CONSEQUENCES   10
Signal showing that lapse has been noticed. If 3 lapses occur, Raymond will be told that he cannot fill in his chart that day.

CONSEQUENCES   11
1. Chart to be filled in and taken home to show parents.
2. 'Special' badge to be worn the next day.
3. 3/5 successful days in a week gives Raymond the right to go to head-master for 'Well done' badge.
4. One extra hour's TV on Friday night.

communicating to Raymond the current situation, seating him in a place where he was least likely to feel disposed to leave his seat and ensuring that he was 'observed' during a lesson where he enjoyed the written work. Again, it can be seen that everything was being done to ensure that Raymond was successful. In the event the arrangements made did ensure him success, but had they not done so, it would have been necessary to look once again at the level of the target and the antecedents.

The 'consequences', i.e. the reinforcement Raymond was to receive, was given very careful consideration and his own preferences were taken fully into account. He enjoyed colouring, cutting out and pasting so his teacher produced a whole range of interesting daily charts for him and he was allowed to complete one of these each day that he achieved his target. She also made a highly decorative 'special' badge for him, which he was able to wear for the remainder of the day on which he completed the target successfully. If he achieved three completed targets in the week, he was allwed to take his three charts to the headmaster who presented him with a 'Well done' badge — something not easily earned in the school. At the end of each day he took his charts home to show his parents so that they could see how he was getting on. Three successfully achieved targets in a week gave him an extra hour of television on Friday night.

Within two to three weeks Raymond achieved his target consistently every day and in discussion with him it was agreed that the time interval could be increased to 45 minutes. Shortly after this, he stopped getting out of his place altogether except for legitimate reasons. It was also interesting that after commencing the programme he stopped wearing the special badge his teacher had made for him as he felt that this 'made him different' from any of the other children. This was significant for a boy who had spent the greater part of his school life apparently going out of his way to do everything calculated to make him different! However, he still treasured the badge although he did not wear it.

Having reached the point where leaving his seat was no longer a problem, the target was changed to the much more difficult one of attempting to bring under control his calling out. It was decided to start off by confining this to the time when his teacher was addressing the whole class — a time when he had always been at his worst. Progressive targets were set again to achieve successive approximations to the behaviour required. Raymond 'had the bit between his teeth' by now and he was clearly enjoying the new-found approbation of his teacher and the headmaster. Good behaviour so obviously paid off that he became almost fully committed to it!

Shortly after the second target had been tackled and achieved,

Figure 15.4: Bar Charts of Raymond's Behaviour

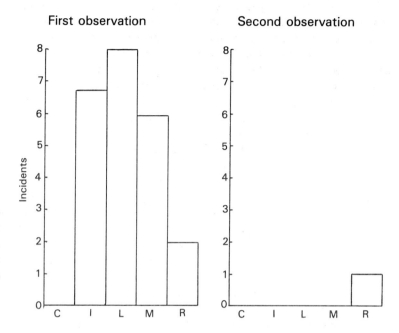

First observation   Second observation

Key: C, calling out; I, inappropriate movement; L, leaving place; M, making noises; R, repetition of instructions

Raymond went away to camp with the school where he behaved in an exemplary manner, enjoyed himself thoroughly and experienced no troubles at all. A few months before, no teacher in the school would have believed this to be possible.

Finally, after a break of about three months when Raymond had moved on to another teacher, an opportunity was taken to carry out a set of observations using exactly the same method as before, at the same time of day and in the same subject. The two sets of results are shown comparatively in Figure 15.4. At a purely subjective level it would have been impossible to have noted Raymond's behaviour as being any different from that of his classmates. There are still occasions when he has some difficulty in exerting full control over himself, notably in long assemblies where he is engaged only in listening. It is possible that a programme will be devised by his teacher to help him with this if he cannot overcome the problem himself. Perhaps the most significant aspect of this case study is that the one behaviour that everyone was convinced 'he could not really help', i.e. making noises, has to all intents and purposes disappeared as a purely incidental spin-off of the control achieved over the other behaviours more amenable to change: an excellent example of generalisation.

Steven T____

Steven was a 10-year-old boy. He lived with his mother, who was separated from Steven's father, and mother's cohabitee. He had a younger half-brother, who was the progeny of his mother's present relationship. There was great rivalry between the two boys and resentment on Steven's part. He enjoyed a very positive relationship with his mother, which was unfortunately marred by some of his behaviours — mostly fighting and temper tantrums. His relationship with Dan, the cohabitee, was not good.

Within school his teacher, Mr Grant, thought that he was of at least average or above average ability. Steven's attainments did not reflect this, being rather below the norm for his class. Mr Grant felt that Steven did just enough work to get by.

When discussing Steven with the psychologist, Mr Grant listed the problems that he was most concerned about. These were: poor peer-group relationships, low work output and being a disruptive influence in class. Discussion clarified exactly what was meant by these descriptions. Disruptive influence in class related to Steven's habit of frequently calling out to the teacher and other children. He also refused to share class equipment. His work output was thought to be low because of the time that he spent in disrupting the class. The description 'poor peer-group relationships' was based on the observation that the other children in the class rejected him. This was thought to be for two main reasons:

(a) his behaviour in class was not accepted by the others;
(b) the other children were frightened of him because of his fighting at breaktimes.

It was then decided that three behaviours should be recorded to establish the severity of the problems. (See Figure 15.5.) The results were as follows:

Calling out comments and answers in class: average 31 times per hour
Refusing to share equipment: 7 to 10 incidents per day
Fighting at breaktimes: 4 out of 10 breaktimes.

Figure 15.5: Assessment Chart, Steven T____

Name of child: Steven T____   Date completed:
Date of birth: Name of teacher:

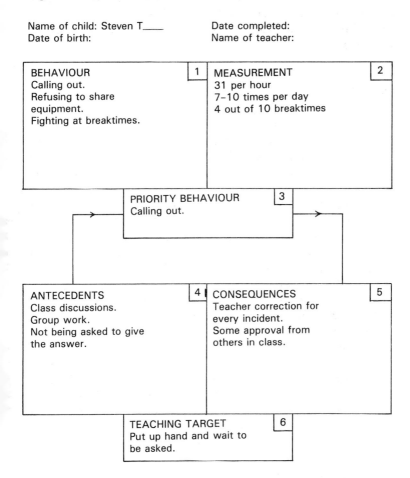

BEHAVIOUR 1	MEASUREMENT 2
Calling out. Refusing to share equipment. Fighting at breaktimes.	31 per hour 7–10 times per day 4 out of 10 breaktimes

PRIORITY BEHAVIOUR 3
Calling out.

ANTECEDENTS 4	CONSEQUENCES 5
Class discussions. Group work. Not being asked to give the answer.	Teacher correction for every incident. Some approval from others in class.

TEACHING TARGET 6
Put up hand and wait to
be asked.

Steven's problems had been noted by a number of teachers in the school and the difficulties had been present for quite some time. Mr Grant decided that it would be advisable to start an intervention (see Figure 15.6) with the behaviour that was most amenable to change in order to prove to everybody that change was possible. He would then go on to tackle the more difficult behaviours once success had been shown. Calling out was the behaviour chosen. Mr Grant also hoped that if this could be reduced it might improve Steven's work output and also improve his image in the eyes of the other children.

Figure 15.6: Intervention Chart, Steven T___

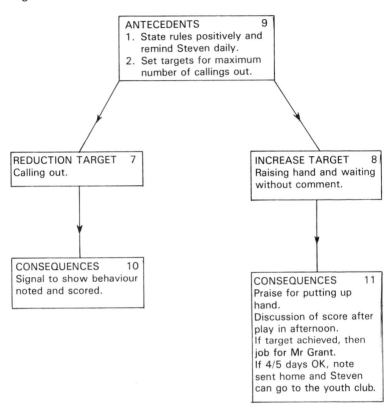

The incidents seemed to occur mostly in class discussion periods and when the class was working quietly in groups. Mr Grant thought that he had been correcting nearly every incident with a remark such as 'Don't call out' or 'Wait until I ask.' There was also some approval for Steven from one or two of the other children in the class whenever this happened.

After discussions with Steven, Mr Grant decided to alter the way in which he handled the problem in the following ways.

(a) He would state the rules positively to Steven and remind him of these each day.

(b) Targets would be set for the maximum numbers of 'calling out' in a given period of time, e.g. a maximum of 15 in an hour.

(c) A score sheet would be kept of the number of times that Steven called out in that time.

(d) If he called out, no verbal reprimand would be given. Instead, a non-verbal sign, a finger raised, would indicate that the behaviour had been noted and scored.

(e) The score would be linked to rewards. If Steven managed to stay within the limits set, then he could go to the headteacher to do a job. This was discussed with Steven and it was clear that this was a highly valued reward.

(f) In addition, if he achieved his target on four out of five days then Mr Grant would send a note home and Steven's mother would let him go to the youth club on Friday evening.

(g) Mr Grant would discuss Steven's performance with him at the end of each afternoon.

(h) A series of steps to target would be used in order to ensure success. The targets would initially be set for a period of one hour. The initial target was to be 15 callings out. Once this was achieved, the target would be successively lowered to 10, to 5, to 2. The length of time over which the targets operated would also be increased from one hour to the whole morning to the whole day. These two variables would be increased singly, e.g. 15 per hour → 10 per hour → 20 per two hours → 5 per hour, etc.

This intervention was almost immediately successful and Mr Grant introduced the idea of Steven recording the incidents himself. The aim was to get Steven to be more aware of his behaviour and to introduce a technique that would be useful later on. This change of approach reduced the number of callings out in a whole day to an average of between 2 and 4. This compared with a total for a whole day of something in the order of 100 incidents before the intervention.

Mr Grant decided to take full advantage of his success and moved on to the problem of the sharing behaviour. Steven used a self-recording diary to keep a record of his behaviour. He had got used to using this with the calling-out recording. He had to record any incidents of being asked to share equipment and whether he co-operated or not. A similar set of targets and reward system were used. This again was quickly successful. Steven was no longer gaining any rewards for following the rules regarding calling out other than regular praise from Mr Grant.

It was then decided to tackle the more difficult problem of fighting. Again a self-recording diary was used. For each breaktime Steven had to record whether or not he had fought with anyone. If he had, then he recorded with whom and what happened before the fight started. The format for the diary was as shown in Figure 15.7.

Figure 15.7: Steven's Diary

DAY		DATE		
Have I had a good breaktime? (No fights)		If I had a fight, who with?		What happened just before I fought?
1				
2				
3				

The aim was to make Steven more aware of the circumstances leading up to a fight and these could then be talked through with Mr Grant. Ways could then be suggested for avoiding the particular incident. (This is an example of using a problem-solving approach to achieve a change in behaviour in which the child plays an active part.) Steven's performance during breaktimes was again linked to a reward system like the calling-out intervention but the headteacher agreed to send a letter home on a Friday if Steven achieved his target for the week.

Incidents of fighting in school dropped to an average of about one a week. Unfortunately there was a reported increase of the number of incidents outside school where it was almost impossible to monitor them. It was not certain if there was an actual increase or whether awareness of them was heightened by the interventions.

A six-month follow-up showed that the improved level of calling out and sharing behaviour had been maintained without the need for reinforcers other than praise and acknowledgement. Fighting was still occurring but almost exclusively out of school. Mr Grant reported that he thought that Steven's relationships with his peers had improved and he now had more friends. Work output was higher than before the intervention but still below the average for the class. Mr Grant thought that this might be the subject for intervention by Steven's next classteacher.

Mary T_____

Mary was seven years old and in a first-year junior class. Her teacher was very concerned about her for although she was not lacking in either ability or attainments, she completed very few tasks in the classroom. The teacher decided to record the number of completed tasks in a week. This came to 3! She next kept a record of the activities that Mary engaged in instead of working. This confirmed a wealth of distracting activities: staring out of the window, sucking pencils and pens, rocking her chair, tapping her ruler, playing with her pony tail, doodling on paper, tapping her feet, etc. All in all, there were too many separate behaviours to contemplate changing each one individually.

The teacher decided that it would be best to attempt to increase the work output directly with the aim of reducing these distracting activities by Mary spending more time working. The teacher designed a programme that was based on 'chunking' the work that Mary had to do into smaller units. This, it was hoped, would allow Mary to see the end of each small task quite easily and thus maintain her concentration. For example, instead of asking Mary to copy 12 lines of work from the board, she would first be asked to copy four lines and come to show the teacher. She would then be asked to complete the next four lines, etc.

On each occasion that she finished one of these short tasks she was praised by the teacher and further reinforced by colouring in a section on a recording chart (Figure 15.8). These were similar in format to the examples at the end of this book. When she completed a chart, she took it home with a 'well done' note from the teacher. Mary and her teacher discussed the design of the charts. She responded very positively to this approach and was soon completing a number of the short tasks within a reasonable time span. The teacher then used a series of steps to target, and increased Mary's work output by two means:

(a) the chunks of work gradually got larger and closer to the standard expected of the other children in the class;
(b) the charts themselves got longer, thus requiring more work to be done in order to complete them.

By combining these two changes Mary's work output increased and she was not as reliant on the reinforcement of the charts. Indeed, after less than a term, Mary's teacher began to fade out the use of the charts by only using them in certain lessons. Soon Mary did not need the charts at all but was sufficiently motivated by the teacher's praise and encouragement to continue working.

Figure 15.8: Recording Chart, Mary T____

Name: *Mary*
Start: *Tuesday, 4th May*
Finish:

Total points: 12

Susan G____

Susan was taken into the care of the local authority at the age of two because of the inability of her parents to care for her adequately. She was under-nourished and neglected and was described as being socially and emotionally deprived. Her parents were given some support during this early period of Susan's life and as she appeared to be missing her mother she was allowed home again for a trial period. In the event the trial proved to be completely unsuccessful and after only a few weeks she was placed with long-term foster parents in an effort to bring some normality into her life.

The foster parents were exceedingly tolerant and patient with the little girl and gradually she became somewhat calmer and more manageable, although she remained excessively dependent and demanding. During her fourth year she was placed in a nursery class at the local primary school where she proved to be noisy, disruptive of other children's play and unable to form relationships with her peer group. Towards her teachers she displayed similar dependent and demanding behaviour to that which she produced at home.

When the time came for her to enter full-time education, it was apparent that the large open-plan primary school to which she would normally have gone was completely unsuited to her needs. Fortunately, there existed in the vicinity a small school which took children up to the age of nine, and with some misgivings the headmistress agreed to take Susan for a trial period. For the first year the teachers worked in close co-operation with the foster parents and in this caring and supportive environment she slowly became more socialised and began to work at school subjects. She was accepted by the other children even though she continued to produce behaviour which was considerably different from the established norms for the school.

By the time Susan attained the age of seven years she was able to produce acceptable work but only in a one-to-one setting. She was able to play co-operatively with the other children but only if they acceded to her wishes. She still found it difficult to engage in activities that were not of her own choosing and she was unable to accept criticism. It was at this stage that a positive behaviour management programme was decided upon, and the following five areas were identified by her teachers as giving rise to the greatest concern:

(a) distracting other children;
(b) not attending to task;

  (c) over-dependence on teacher;
  (d) immature verbal behaviour;
  (e) inappropriately loud speech.

Problem area (e) was chosen because it was felt that it would respond successfully and reasonably quickly to the positive behaviour management approach. Furthermore it was seen as a 'springboard' from which the more serious problems might be tackled.

Susan delighted in being given the task of taking messages from one teacher to another, and on these occasions she would announce the nature of her business in a loud voice to each class which she passed through to deliver her message. It was decided to allow Susan to carry out a cutting and pasting task (an activity which was highly prized by her) directly following each occasion when she carried a message in silence through the other classrooms and delivered it quietly to the teacher. The programme was explained to Susan, and her teachers ensured that there were at least two occasions each day when she was asked to carry messages. This programme was immediately and wholly successful, Susan never failing to achieve her reward.

After a period of two weeks, it was decided to adopt a new target behaviour while retaining the initial one reinforced only by praise, with the material reward being transferred to the new target behaviour. This was 'not attending to task' and it promised to be rather less amenable to rapid change than the first, especially as the increase target was defined as 'attention to task outside a one-to-one setting'. It will be recalled that until this time Susan had proved to be incapable of producing work outside this setting. Clearly, a shaping approach was indicated for this programme, as the norm for the group in subjects such as number and creative writing was well beyond her reach. This norm was judged to be about 15 minutes so Susan's target behaviour was set at this level; however, the first 'step to target' was set at only 2 minutes. It can readily be seen that this programme contained considerable scope for adjustment and 'fine tuning' as it could be applied to a whole variety of tasks, to different times of the day, to different time intervals and to differing numbers of intervals during the day.

The intervals were measured using a large minute-timer, set and started by the teacher with the onus placed on Susan to indicate by raising her hand that the interval had ended. Within a few weeks she had achieved the norm for the class and, not surprisingly, her work had improved greatly and in some subjects she had attained a level which was acceptable for her age. It was also interesting to note that although she still loved to cut and paste, she relinquished this reward at her own request.

At the age of five Susan might well have been placed in a special school for children with moderate learning difficulties. She has, in fact, been able to remain in mainstream education and there is good reason to predict that this will remain the case.

Brian P____

Brian was a 13-year-old boy attending his local comprehensive school. He had quite a history of causing problems within school and had recently been suspended following a fight in the playground. Soon after Brian returned to school, his tutor called a meeting of all the teachers who taught him. At the meeting it was quite apparent that although there was a lot of ill feeling among the staff about some of Brian's behaviour, most teachers had quite a liking for him. It was clear that they would like to see him succeed on his return to the school.

The meeting discussed the behaviours that they thought were the most difficult to cope with and listed them:

(a) making noises — aeroplanes, cars, hooters, etc.;
(b) hitting other pupils in class;
(c) swearing in class;
(d) fighting in the playground.

The teachers decided that they would record the number of occasions on which Brian made noises, swore and hit other pupils during the next week. They felt that it was not necessary to record the incidents of fighting as these were already logged in the school's record system — at least all the ones which were reported. They also agreed to try to identify exactly what happened before and after each incident so that they could plan an intervention strategy at their next meeting.

At the next meeting the results were discussed. It appeared that Brian made noises in almost every lesson during the week on an average of two to four times per lesson. There were only two incidents of swearing and none of hitting other children. The staff commented that these figures were probably an underestimate as Brian still appeared to be 'on his best behaviour' following his suspension. However, a clear pattern for his behaviour emerged. This seemed to be:

Brian makes a noise → other pupils tease him or make comments → Brian makes comments in return → further comments → Brian swears at or hits the pupil concerned.

This could then lead to confrontations with the teachers as Brian often denied what he had done. It appeared that he was very unwilling to acknowledge his own behaviour.

It was decided that it was very important to make Brian more aware of his behaviour and its consequences in order to develop more self-control. The following intervention was suggested for discussion with Brian and his parents.

(a) Any intervention should be formalised by means of a contract.
(b) The behaviour to be concentrated on at first should be making noises as this seemed to be the first link in a chain of events. Stopping this should prevent many of the other behaviours.
(c) A self-recording system should be used on a lesson-by-lesson basis indicating whether or not Brian had made any noises, or sworn at or hit any pupils.
(d) The record should be checked by the teacher at the end of each lesson.
(e) A target should be set for Brian each week.
(f) His performance in school could be linked to some reinforcement at home.
(g) The teachers would give Brian positive reinforcement if he had a successful lesson and suggest alternative actions if he had not achieved his target. Above all they would seek to avoid confrontations within class by either discussing the matter after the lesson when they checked Brian's record or by giving Brian a brief cooling-off period with his tutor or the head of pastoral care.
(h) Brian's tutor would see him on a regular basis to discuss his progress. This should be daily at the start of the intervention but tailing off to weekly if progress was achieved.

Brian's tutor arranged to meet with Brian and his parents. At this meeting the proposed intervention was discussed and a final version was agreed. This was summarised in the contract shown in Figure 15.9.

This intervention led to a dramatic reduction in the within-lesson problems but troubles still continued at breaktimes. A further intervention was instituted the following term which had some limited success in reducing the number of fights but not in eliminating them altogether.

Figure 15.9: Brian's Contract

This is a contract between Brian, Mum, Dad and Mr Walters to help Brian behave better in school. We have all discussed and agreed the following conditions.

(1) Brian will use his diary every lesson and record how well he thinks he has behaved (1 = badly, up to 5 = very well). He will also note if he has made any noises.

(2) Brian will try not to make any noises in lessons, especially planes, hooters, etc.

(3) At the end of the lesson Brian will show the diary to his teacher who will note if he agrees or disagrees with Brian's mark and put in his own mark.

(4) At the end of the day Brian will take his diary to Mr Walters. They will count up the score and talk about how well Brian has done and any problems.

(5) Brian will take his diary home every day and show it to his Mum. If he has reached his target for the day, then Mum will give him 20p of his pocket money. If he hasn't, then he will not get his pocket money that day.

(6) If Brian reaches the target on 4 or 5 days in a week, then Dad will take him out in his van on Saturday.

Starting date: 4 November   Signed: Brian
Review date: 11 November   Dad
Finishing date: 18 November   Mum
                                      Mr Walters

Darren H____

Darren had been a cause for concern to his teachers over a period of time extending right back to his early days in the primary school. He was small in stature and he had been variously described as immature, disruptive, hyperactive and uncontrolled. In the primary school he was placed in a small remedial group of ten children which he attended on a full-time basis. Although he had the reputation of producing quite bizarre behaviour, for example hiding under desks, inappropriate noises, walking out of lessons, etc., this was quite powerfully rewarded as he was seen as being the 'class clown' both by the children and the teachers. He was amusedly tolerated in the primary school but this situation changed quite dramatically upon his transfer to secondary school education and his placement in a mainstream class. In spite of being of average intellectual ability as evidenced by his good reading and general grasp of concepts, he was unprepared to work, to conform to the norms of the school or to relinquish his clowning.

At about this time a short course on positive behaviour management had been mounted in the school which was attended by about a third of the staff. Sufficient interest had been generated for a group of teachers to agree to attempt to initiate a programme for Darren. This was grasped almost as 'a last straw' in view of the failure of a whole series of punitive measures to bring about any lasting change in Darren's behaviour.

It was pointed out that for a programme to be successful it would be necessary for all the teachers who dealt with Darren, or at least a significant majority of them, to agree to adopt the measures contained in the programme to ensure a consistency of approach.

The main areas of concern were identified as:

(a) limited physical aggression towards other pupils;
(b) verbal aggression towards staff and pupils;
(c) bizarre, attention-seeking behaviour;
(d) extreme disorganisation (never prepared for lessons with the appropriate equipment).

It was decided to place Darren in a remedial group in order that he would have contact with a reduced number of staff. The target behaviour chosen for modification was the physical and verbal aggression, and although a material reward consisting of extra opportunities for reading was offered to him, much greater emphasis was placed on social rewards, e.g. praise and teacher approval. Needless to say, Darren's experience of the latter was extremely limited.

Within the supportive setting of the remedial group the programme was successful but there remained the problem of his ability to generalise this behaviour to a mainstream situation. This was overcome by one teacher from the remedial department taking on the role of co-ordinator. This involved consulting personally at the end of each teaching session with all the teachers who had taken Darren, and discussing their comments with him each day. He was, therefore, still receiving a great deal of the attention he craved but in a much more positive way. The bizarre behaviour, which had been regarded as Darren's most difficult problem, was never tackled directly because it became automatically extinguished as he began to receive reinforcement for appropriate behaviour.

However, Darren's generally disorganised approach to school work remained a contentious issue. This became the subject of a contract which was drawn up by the educational psychologist in full consultation with Darren and his teachers. It had been discovered that Darren greatly enjoyed gardening and was also a member of a model-making club conducted after school. Darren was prepared to make a great effort to achieve participation in both these activities, and schedules were devised that enabled him to earn these activities as rewards. Before long, 'perfect' days were being reported, which earned the additional reinforcement of being sought out by the headteacher to receive praise. A truly unique experience for Darren!

Janet R___

Janet was a bright 6-year-old whose attainments were above average. She would have been a pleasure to have had in any class but for one thing — temper tantrums. Janet did not like to be disturbed from her current activity to change to another. In fact, she often refused to stop what she was doing when her teacher asked her to. If the teacher pressed the point, then she would lose her temper, shout, cry and even throw things.

Her teacher looked very carefully at the antecedent events and her own behaviour before deciding on the following course of action:

(a) She would state the rules clearly to Janet and rehearse them in private.

(b) Before giving any instructions to the class, she would walk to a position close to Janet's desk.

(c) The instructions would be phased. First, the class would be told to stop what they were doing and to put down everything that they had in their hands. This ensured a physical break of activity. Then the class would be told what they would be doing next.

(d) The class requests would be personalised for Janet so that she could not misunderstand that they were meant for her as well.

(e) She was to be given one reminder and then the material that she was using would be removed by the teacher.

(f) If there was any shouting or loss of temper, then a time-out procedure would be initiated.

(g) If Janet changed activities without fuss, then the teacher praised
her and reminded her of what she had done to deserve the praise.

These simply rearranged antecedents proved to be very successful quite
quickly. The time-out procedure was used on only two occasions in the
first two weeks of the programme and not at all after that. This compared favourably with the baseline incidence of temper tantrums of at
least six to eight a week.

Janet's teacher was delighted with the progress achieved by this simple intervention and after a month did not regard Janet as her major problem in the class.

16 TEN POINTS TO REMEMBER

1. *Be specific.* Say exactly what the child *does*, not a 'vague' description of the behaviour.

2. *Be accurate.* Do measure the behaviour. This way you will be able to make the right choice of target and be able to see improvement, which is important for both you and the child.

3. *Talk to each other.* Discuss what you intend to do and why with the child as seems appropriate. If you can enlist his co-operation, then the programme is much more likely to succeed.

4. *Be consistent.* Once you have stated the rules to the child (i.e. what level of behaviour, what the rewards/punishments will be and when they will be given), don't compromise — stick to your guns.

5. *Be positive.* Catch the child being good. Try to ignore the negative side of his behaviour (if you can). This is the strategy of praise/ignoring.

6. *Be a reward giver.* Rather than punish inappropriate behaviour, reward behaviour that is incompatible with that which would be punished. For example, praise a child for sitting down rather than admonish him for standing up.

THINK ABOUT IT.

7. *Don't despair.* There will be practical problems. For example, what we at first think may be rewarding may turn out not to be so. Care may be needed with reward-giving with respect to the other members of the class.

8. *Things may get worse.* Before they get better. It is often the case that the inappropriate behaviour increases (testing you out) before it decreases under the effect of the programme.

9. *Rome wasn't built in a day.* Don't expect radical changes overnight — settle for small steps towards the ultimate goal.

10. *Don't think the worst of the child.* Look at the other children in the class and compare their behaviour with that of the child in question (that is, don't ask him/her to be an angel).

APPENDIX: SAMPLE CHARTS

(1) An Example of a Contract Form

> ### BEHAVIOUR CONTRACT
>
> Behaviour contract for:
> With and between:
>
> Starting Date:
> Review Date:
> Finishing Date:
>
> TARGET BEHAVIOURS:
>
>
> BONUS:
>
>
> PENALTY:
>
> We the undersigned have discussed and agreed the attached conditions:
>
> _____ Pupil   _____ Teacher
> _____ Parent(s) _____ Headteacher
>
> _____

(2) An Example of an ABC Recording Chart

DATE	TIME	BEHAVIOUR What happened?	ANTECEDENTS What happened before?	CONSEQUENCES What happened after?

(3) Some Examples of Recording Charts for Primary Children

Name:
Start:
Finish:

Total
Points: 24

19	20	21	22	23	24
13	14	15	16	17	18
7	8	9	10	11	12
1	2	3	4	5	6

BMF

Name:
Start:
Finish:

Total Points: 10

Name:
Start:
Finish:

Total
Points: 20

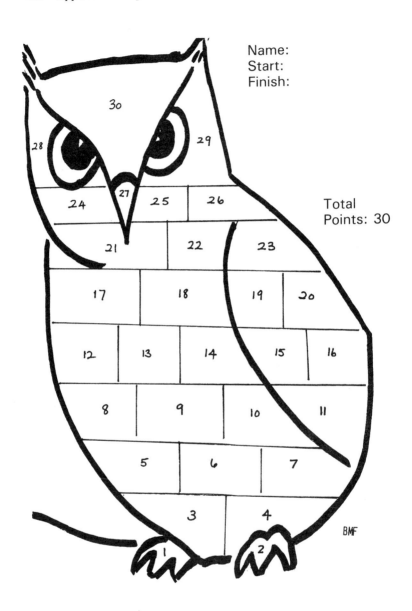

Name:
Start:
Finish:

Total
Points: 30

SUGGESTIONS FOR FURTHER READING

G.J. Blackham and A. Silberman (1975) *Modification of Child and Adolescent Behaviour*, 2nd edn, Wadsworth Publishing Co., Monterey, California

Marg Csapo (1975) *Beat the Hassle — A Survival Kit for Teenagers and their Parents*, Centre for Human Development and Research, Vancouver, Canada

Marg Csapo (1978) *Pocketful of Praises — A Handbook for Parents*, 3rd edn, Centre for Human Development and Research, Vancouver, Canada

Marg Csapo (1978) *Glue Him Down — Teaching Hyperactive Children*, Centre for Human Development and Research, Vancouver, Canada

Marg Csapo (1979) *Put a Feather in Your Cap — Self Management for Teachers*, Centre for Human Development and Research, Vancouver, Canada

William J. DeRisi and George Butz (1975) *Writing Behavioural Contracts*, Research Press, Springfield, Illinois

Martin Herbert (1981) *Behavioural Treatment of Problem Children — A Practical Manual*, Academic Press, London/Grune & Stratton, New York

Lloyd Homme (1970) *How to Use Contingency Contracting in the Classroom*, Research Press, Springfield, Illinois

Robert Laslett and Colin Smith (1984) *Effective Classroom Management*, Croom Helm, London/Nichols Publishing Company, New York

James A. Poteet (1973/1974) *Behaviour Modification — Practical Guide for Teachers*, Burgess Publishing Co., Hodder & Stoughton, London

John Robertson (1981) *Effective Classroom Control*, Hodder & Stoughton, London

Julie S. Vargas (1977) *Behavioural Psychology for Teachers*, Harper & Row, New York

E.V.S. Westmacott and R.J. Cameron (1981) *Behaviour Can Change*, Globe Education, London

K. Wheldall, D. Wheldall and S. Winter (1983) *Seven Supertactics for Superparents*, NFER-Nelson, Windsor

Ted Wragg (1981) *Class Management and Control — A Teaching Skills Workbook*, Macmillan Education, London

INDEX